WEAVING A TAPESTRY

Loneliness, Spiritual Well-Being, and Communal Support

Carol A. Wintermyer

UNIVERSITY
PRESS OF
AMERICA

Lanham • New York • London

Copyright © 1993 by
University Press of America®, Inc.
4720 Boston Way
Lanham, Maryland 20706

3 Henrietta Street
London WC2E 8LU England

Library of Congress Cataloging-in-Publication Data

Wintermyer, Carol A.
Weaving a tapestry : loneliness, spiritual well-being, and communal
support / Carol A. Wintermyer.
p.   cm.
Includes bibliographical references and indexes.
1. Monastic and religious life of women—Psychology.
2. Loneliness—Religious aspects—Catholic Church.   3. Nuns—
Social networks.   4. Social networks—Psychological aspects—Case
studies.   5. Loneliness—Case studies.   I. Title.
BX4205.W56   1993   248.8'943—dc20   93–16058 CIP

ISBN 0–8191–9179–5 (cloth : alk. paper)

 The paper used in this publication meets the minimum requirements of
American National Standard for Information Sciences—Permanence
of Paper for Printed Library Materials, ANSI Z39.48–1984.

IN LOVING MEMORY
OF
LIONEL PARENTEAU

ACKNOWLEDGMENTS

I would like to thank all those who supported and encouraged me throughout my work on this manuscript. Merle Jordan, Th.D. and Carole Bohn Ed.D., my primary readers, were so helpful and most supportive of me throughout this entire process. I thank my very good friend, Jean Morrow, Ed.D., who supported and worked with me as a statistical consultant. I thank Dr. Dan Russell and Dr. Craig Ellison for permission to use their respective instruments in this study. I thank my friends and colleagues from Boston University whose support throughout my work was ever present. I thank the Sisters of Mercy who have supported me and encouraged me to pursue my education to better serve others with mercy and compassion. In a very special way I thank Dr. Nancy Kehoe and Dr. Jane Bain who have helped me more and more to believe in myself. And most especially, I thank my brother Bob and sister-in-law Ruth, for without their support this work would not be possible.

TABLE OF CONTENTS

LIST OF ILLUSTRATIONS

LIST OF TABLES

INTRODUCTION

A wish to offer a study of substance that would be of benefit to women belonging to religious congregation led me to explore the phenomena of loneliness. As I explored loneliness it became apparent that it was related to spiritual well-being ad social\communal support. Based upon this discovery, a study was designed to measure loneliness in relationship to spiritual well-being and communal support from 1960 to the present in women belonging to religious congregations within the Roman Catholic tradition.

The first facet was to measure loneliness, spiritual well-being and communal support in the present. To measure these phenomena in the present, The Spiritual Well-Being Scale developed by Ellison, 1982; the UCLA Loneliness Scale (Version 3) developed by Russell and Cutrona, 1984, and network lists modeled on Hirsch (1980) and Stokes (1985) were used and through statistical analysis studied the impact that spiritual well-being and communal support had upon loneliness within this population. It will become apparent in the text of this study that there is a significant relationship between loneliness, spiritual well-being, and some facets of communal support.

While loneliness scores tended to be low and spiritual well-being scores high, the loneliness experienced by the women in this study was found to be strongly related to spiritual well-being, existential well-being, and religious well-being. This loneliness can result in an inability to discover meaning and purpose in one's life, a feeling of unconnectedness to self, other, God, and a sense that one does not belong to a significant network whether communal and/or personal. Spiritual well-being, for many, appears to enable the individual to cope with loneliness, drawing on an intimate relationship with God.

The second facet studied these phenomena from 1960 to the present. Religious life has undergone many changes over the last three decades. This study offers a lens through which we can view loneliness, spiritual well-being, and communal support in the context of leadership style, and method of determining one's place of residence. Each sister was asked to rate their experiences of these phenomena for each place of residence from 1960 - the present. This too offers data supporting a significant relationship between loneliness, spiritual well-being and communal support, and gives some evidence that a collegial style of leadership and a personal choice for places of residence lead to a greater sense of overall-well-being for the individual.

In viewing loneliness among sisters, loss was named as a significant issue. With the many transitions in religious life as a result of Vatican II, the uncertainty of how religious life will look in the future and an increasing aging population is cause for concern within religious congregations.

This study not only is of significance to religious congregation of women, but also adds to the research in the fields of loneliness, spiritual well-being, and communal/ support networks. This study on loneliness furthers the research of Russell, Peplau, and Cutrona[1] by using the UCLA Loneliness Scale (Version 3) in a non-student population. Targeting a large population of women religious enhances the theoretical and applied knowledge about the experience of loneliness.

The study also furthers the research of Paloutzian and Ellison[2] on spiritual well-being, and addresses Moberg[3] expressing the need for psychologists to study the phenomenon of spiritual well-being as it pertains to wellness or health of the totality of our inner resources. This study offers further validation of their instrument with conceptually related measures; i.e., loneliness and social support. While Paloutzian et al. have established norms for the spiritual well-being of a number of religious groups, none have been done with religious congregations of women. This study adds a dimension to their body of research by looking at a group of women who have made a public profession of their commitment to God, their congregation, and the Church as a whole.

By viewing conceptual entities that affect our sense of wellness, namely loneliness, social/communal support and spiritual well-being, one finds that these entities are not discrete phenomena but are integrally connected to one another.

---

[1] Dan Russell et al., "The revised UCLA loneliness scale: Concurrent and discriminant validity evidence,"Journal of Personality and Social Psychology 39 (1980): 472-480.

[2] Raymond Paloutzian and Craig Ellison, "Loneliness, Spiritual Well-Being and the Quality of Life," in Loneliness: A sourcebook of current theory, research and therapy eds. Letitia Peplau and Dan Perlman (New York: John Wiley & Sons, 1982), 224-237.

[3] David Moberg, "The Development of Social Indicators of Spiritual Well-Being for Quality of Life Research," in Spiritual well-being: Sociological perspectives, ed. David Moberg (University Press of America: Washington, D.C., 1979), 1-13.

CHAPTER ONE

BUILDING THE TAPESTRY

Loneliness is an experience that is interwoven into our life experience from birth, an experience that is often frightening. It touches our lives at different times and for different reasons. Fromm-Reichmann tells us that "anyone who has encountered persons who were under the influence of real loneliness understands why people are more frightened of being lonely than being hungry, or being deprived of sleep, or of having their sexual needs unfulfilled."[1] In the midst of loneliness one can experience alienation from self, other, God, and that which gives meaning to life. In society today we see a high level of this alienation combined with a strong search for personal fulfillment, security, inner peace, and an increased concern for spiritual phenomena; in particular, spiritual well-being.[2] In the seeking we are drawn to others who will form a bond and common vision in order to feel a part of or belong to a group of significant others.

Loneliness

Loneliness is an experience that is common to most everyone[3] and is "most often regarded as a negative, depressing aspect of human existence."[4] "Data on the prevalence of loneliness in the general population is fairly consistent across a number of large studies. Less than 10 percent of the population report that they have never been lonely; and in most studies, this figure is more likely to be around 1 or 2 percent."[5] "While loneliness is a given for human life and, therefore, a companion in every relationship"[6], it is one that we avoid and deny because of the pain and fear it engenders in our lives.[7]

---

[1] Frieda Fromm-Reichmann, "Loneliness," in The Anatomy of Loneliness, eds. J. Hartog and Y. Cohen (New York: International Universities Press,1980), 348.

[2] Moberg, 1979.

[3] Perlman et al., 1982; Jeanne George, "Loneliness in the Priesthood," Human Development 10 (1989): 12-15; Loire Hsu et al., "Cultural and Emotional Components of Loneliness and Depression," The Journal of Psychology 121 (1986): 61-70; Janice Williams and Cecilia Solano, The Social Reality of Feeling Lonely: Friendship and Reciprocation, Personality and Social Psychology Bulletin 9 (1983): 237-242.

[4] Karen Cioffi, "Loneliness: A painful blessing," Spiritual Life 34 (1988): 144.

[5] George, 12.

[6] Paula Ripple, "Saying Yes to Life: Saying Yes to Relationships," Studies in Formative Spirituality 6 (1985): 393.

[7] Fromm-Reichmann; Clark Moustakas, Loneliness (New York: Prentice Hall, Inc, 1961); Henry Stack Sullivan, "The Interpersonal Theory of Psychiatry," in The Interpersonal Theory of Psychiatry, eds. Helen Swick Perry and Mabel Gawel (New York: W. W. Norton and

Weiss cites Fromm-Reichmann as saying, "Many of us severely underestimate our own past experience with loneliness, and as a result, underestimate the role it has played in the lives of others."[8] Though it is a pervasive human experience, the pain of loneliness causes one to avoid it, counter it, or correct it.[9] Given that loneliness is a phenomenon that tends to be ignored, and at the same time appears to be somewhat pervasive in society, merits study.

"Loneliness appears always to be a response to the absence of some particular type of relationship or, more accurately, a response to the absence of some particular relational provision."[10] Emotional isolation, according to Weiss, occurs in the absence of a close emotional attachment to another and is dominated by anxiety and apprehension. This has its roots in early childhood. It is a re-experiencing of the anxiety produced by childhood abandonment. This notion is supported by Bowlby, a noted theorist on separation-anxiety. Separation anxiety and the capacity for the infant to bond affectively with another affects greatly one's ability to attain and maintain a sense of health and well-being as an adult. Bowlby states:

> A great many forms of psychiatric disorders can be understood as resulting from the malfunctioning of a person's capacity to make and to maintain affectional bonds with particular others; patterns on which a person's affectional bonds are modeled during adult life are determined to a significant degree by events within his family of origin during childhood . . . .[11]

Based on the thought that loneliness is in part the result of separation anxiety, Parkes maintains that it (loneliness) is triggered by a loss or separation of some kind which taps into the experience of separation-anxiety experienced as an infant.[12] This experience of separation from

Company, 1953).
    [8] Weiss, 12.
    [9] Myer Mendelson, "Reflections on Loneliness," Contemporary Psychoanalysis 26 (1990): 330-354.
    [10] Weiss, 17.
    [11] John Bowlby, "Affectional Bonds," in Loneliness: The Experience of Emotional and Social Isolation, ed. Robert Weiss (Cambridge: MIT Press,1973), 38.
    [12] C. Murray Parkes, Separation Anxiety: An Aspect of the Search of the Lost Object, in Loneliness: The Experience of Emotional and Social Isolation, Robert Weiss, ed, (Cambridge: MIT Press, 1973) 53-68.

others is universal and is probably the most commonly recognized feature of loneliness.[13] This loss of the significant other(s) creates a sense of emotional estrangement or abandonment.[14] This again leads to "feelings of anxiety, fear, and concern about present and future existence."[15]

This sense of isolation takes on a social dimension. According to Weiss, this dimension, referred to as social isolation, is demonstrated through the absence of an engaging social network. It is marked by "feelings of boredom or aimlessness, together with feelings of marginality."[16] In the social dimension of loneliness, an individual affectively perceives that s/he has been pushed out of a significant group to which the person belongs.[17] This corresponds to the feeling of being separated from valued group interactions which have the potential to engender appreciation, approval, and feelings of self-esteem. Social isolation can be viewed as the absence of those positive things.[18] This loneliness can be characterized by a lack of assurance that one belongs or is wanted by others.[19]

Peplau et al. suggest that when a person's social relations are not at their optimum, s/he experiences the stress of loneliness. "Loneliness is the unpleasant experience that occurs when a person's network of social relations is deficient in some important way, either quantitatively or qualitatively."[20] The evaluations of these relationships are influenced by past experiences, cultural and situational factors, and the cognitive processes concerning people's perception and evaluation of their social relations. Past experience leads us to develop images of the kinds of social interactions that make us feel happy and satisfied, and those that do not.

---

[13] Rokach, "Theoretical Approaches."

[14] Ami Rokach, "The Experience of Loneliness: A Tri-level model," The Journal of Psychology 122 (1988): 531-543; Robert Neale, Loneliness, Solitude, and Companionship (Philadelphia: Westminister Press, 1984); Lars Andersen, "A Model of Estrangement: Including a Theoretical Understanding of Loneliness," Psychological Reports 58 (1986): 683-695.

[15] Rokach, "Experience of Loneliness," 538.

[16] Weiss, 22.

[17] Rokach, "Theoretical Approaches"; Romeo Bonsaint, "Loneliness: A Social-Developmental Analysis," Studies in Formative Spirituality 5 (1984): 323-333.

[18] Andersen.

[19] Craig Ellison, "Loneliness: A Social-Developmental Analysis," Journal of Psychology and Theology 6 (1978): 3-16.

[20] Peplau et al., 4.

We rate our interpersonal relations in comparison to those of other people.[21]

Harry Stack Sullivan looks at the importance of attachment, acceptance, and need for the other and describes loneliness as a "terribly important component of personality."[22]   Loneliness is for him "the exceedingly unpleasant and driving experience connected with inadequate discharge of the need for human intimacy, for interpersonal intimacy."[23] He looks at loneliness from a developmental model and moves beyond the experience of separation-anxiety as an infant. The components that culminate in the experience of loneliness are fourfold. It first appears in infancy as a need for contact with the other. This continues into childhood where the need for the adult participation in the child's activities is very important. As a juvenile the need for peers and peer acceptance is very strong, and in preadolescence the need to have someone with whom intimate exchanges can occur is vital. It is at this level, according to Sullivan[24], that loneliness reaches its full significance and changes little into adulthood. When these needs are thwarted and deficient, loneliness arises. These deficits create tremendous anxiety within the person, and demonstrate that loneliness in itself is even more terrible than anxiety. Ellison's developmental factors parallel Sullivan's components. Ellison cites three developmental needs, attachment, acceptance, and acquisition of adequate social skills. If these factors are not met, the person would develop a chronic experience of loneliness.[25]

Each of the forms of loneliness discussed thus far can bring about a sense of self-alienation that describes "a feeling of inner void, a detachment from one's self, and an alienation from one's core identity."[26] In this as well as a "foreignness to one's surroundings . . . the individual becomes trapped in silence and incommunicability."[27] The person feels

---

[21] Letitia Peplau, Maria Miceli, and Bruce Morasch, "Loneliness and Self-Evaluation," in Loneliness: A Sourcebook of Current Theory, Research and Therapy, eds.   Letitia Peplau and Dan Perlman (New York: John Wiley & Sons, 1982), 135-151.

[22] Sullivan, 261.

[23] Ibid. 290.

[24] Ibid.

[25] Ellison.

[26] Rokach, "Experience of Loneliness", 534.

[27] Jeffrey Sobosan, "Loneliness and Faith," Journal of Psychology and Theology 6 (1978): 104.

him/herself, to some degree, unaccepted by the world, and when s/he reaches out, there is an inability to make contact. "In loneliness one is definitely alone, cut off from human companionship."[28] This isolation is not only from self and others, but can be from God as well.

It touches all facets of life, the emotional, social and spiritual. It impacts one's relationship to self, other, and God. While one may deny its existence, it is inevitable that feeling lonely will be a part of life.

Social Networks/Support

Given that loneliness is a part of one's life and that social relationships or their absence are considered an aspect of one's experience of loneliness, it is important to explore one's social networks to understand more fully the phenomenon of loneliness.

This study looks at the social dimension of human experience, specifically by looking at social networks and social support and, even more particularly, by looking at community social support as found in religious congregations of Roman Catholic women. Social network analysis has significant implications for understanding community life and for enabling one to develop programs that can lead to more healthy living within the community.[29]

The criteria for being a member of a social network vary from author to author. Mitchell et al. cite several definitions; i.e., the primary group as being made up of all kin, nominated friends, work associates, and neighbors; all the people who are important in your life at this moment, whether you like them or not.[30] Hirsch defines it as a matrix formed by up to 15 significant others with whom one is likely to interact at least once during any two-week period.[31] The particular interaction referred to here is that of social support.

There is a growing consensus among theorists that social support, "an exchange of resources between at least two individuals perceived by the

---

[28] Moustakas, 47.
[29] Ibid.
[30] Mitchell et al.
[31] Hirsch.

provider or the recipient to be intended to enhance the well-being of the recipient"[32], is found to have a definite impact upon an individual's sense of health and well-being.[33] This is supported by many other sources.[34] Heller et al. tell us that the best predictors of this are network size, frequency of church attendance, and proportion of network members considered intimates.[35] The exact mechanisms for how social ties and support influence health and well-being are not clear. It is clear, however, that the multidimensional nature of support is present.[36]

"During the past decade, support system research successfully demonstrated that health is related, as well, to the availability of supportive ties, e.g., the number of ties in a social network, the frequency of contact with network members, and the differential presence of kin or friends in these networks".[37] Along with this, one must keep in mind the need of looking at relationships that are not necessarily supportive.[38] Including in the analysis network supportive, non-supportive, or neutral relationships enables one to study more effectively the complex nature of one's ties and networks. Varying types of relationships may provide different types of support. Therefore it would be important to classify these relationships by category as well as by their content.

One must look at social/communal support from a number of vantage points; i.e., source, structure, and function.[39] The source looks at

---

[32] Schumaker et al., 13.

[33] Mitchell et al.; Kenneth Heller and William E. Mansbach, "The Multifaceted Nature of Social Support in a Community Sample of Elderly Women," Journal of Social Issues 40 (1984): 99-112; Wellman; Karen Rook, "Research on Social Support, Loneliness, and Social Isolation," Review of Personality and Social Psychology, 5 (1984): 239-264.

[34] Donald Unger and Abraham Wandersman, "The Importance of Neighbors: The Social, Cognitive, and Affective Components of Neighboring," American Journal of Community Psychology 13 (1985): 139-169; Joseph Stokes, "The Relation of Social Network and Individual Differences to Loneliness," Journal of Personality and Social Psychology 48 (1985): 981-990; Arlene Brownell and Sally Ann Shumaker, "Social Support: An Introduction to a Complex Phenomenon," Journal of Social Issues 40 (1984): 1-9; Rina Alcalay, "Health and Social Support Networks: A Case for Improving Interpersonal Communications," Social Networks 5 (1983): 71-88.

[35] Heller et al.

[36] Wellman.

[37] Ibid. 172.

[38] Ibid; Shinn et al.

[39] Shinn et al.

the category of the relationship such as friend, kin, or colleague. The structure looks at such aspects as density, size, strength of ties,[40] and the number of independent contacts among persons in the network.[41] The function of social support consists of such features as health sustenance and stress reduction, as well as a maintenance and enhancement of self-identity and self-esteem. The density of a network, where members are highly interconnected, would be "cohesive, strong, and effective support systems . . . . Higher density networks produce more support than lower density networks."[42] Israel and Antonucci discovered that network size was found to be a significant predictor of life satisfaction.[43] The smaller the size of the reference group becomes, the greater the sense of cohesiveness and sense of belonging,[44] especially when the group is a self-selected group.

The presence of social/communal support networks implies that there exists a sharing history with significant others through permanence and commitment to long-lasting relationships; through providing an environment of support, particularly in times of need; and through not using others as a means for achieving goals.[45] When social support is deficient there are marked consequences. Loneliness is one of those consequences. It has been found to be negatively related to social support[46], informing us that when one's social relationships differ from what is desired, loneliness occurs.[47] Long term deficits in social networks are more crippling and may lead to chronic and persistent loneliness.[48]

Authors such as Hirsch refer to our social network as a personal

---

[40] Barton Hirsch, "Social Networks and the Coping Process: Creating Personal Communities," in Social Networks and Social Support, ed. Benjamin Gottleib (Beverly Hills: Sage Publications, 1981), 149-170.

[41] Alcalay.

[42] Stokes, 142.

[43] Barbara Israel and Toni Antonucci, "Social Network Characteristics and Psychological Well-Being: A Replication and Extension," Health Education Quarterly 14 (1987): 461-481.

[44] Patrick Moffet, "Marginality and Religious Life: Belonging to a Group Called to Risk," Review for Religious 43 (1984): 842-848.

[45] Alcalay.

[46] Michael Newcomb and Peter Bentler, "Loneliness and Social Support: A Confirmatory Hierarchical Analysis, Personality and Social Psychology Bulletin 12 (1986): 520-535.

[47] Rook.

[48] Ami Rokach, "Antecedents of Loneliness: A Factorial Analysis," Journal of Psychology 123 (1989): 369-384.

community that reflects our involvement in the major spheres of our life.[49] It is these communities that create and maintain a meaningful participation in society. Personal communities seldom have well defined boundaries. There is no way to clearly define members from non-members.[50] Personal social networks provide access to resources that are important to the well-being of the individual as well as the community itself.[51] "In particular they provide helping resources which exist naturally in people's social networks."[52] They provide access to resources which are important not only for the individual's sense of well-being, but also for the well-being of the internal functioning of the community.[53] Each person is regarded as the central point of a potentially complex network of community ties.

While the boundaries of a personal community may not be clearly defined, and membership difficult to determine by category, corporate communities to which one belongs such as towns, churches, families, and religious congregations have definite boundaries. Unger et al. cite four elements developed by McMillan and Chavis for a sense of community: membership, influence, sharing of values, and shared emotional connection. Membership involves a feeling of belonging, and a sense of relatedness with the following attributes: (a) recognized boundaries which define who belongs; (b) emotional safety; (c) sense of belonging and identification with the group; (d) personal investment which involves active participation in the group; and (e) common symbol systems which involve the holding of similar language, rituals, ceremonies, or other signs of commonality.[54] The nature of the broader community may be expected to have an impact on the nature of the individual's social network. This will happen in relationship to the person's experience of community, and the individual's participation in community processes. "Influence involves whether the individual can influence the group; whether the group has influence on the individual and can put pressure on the individual to conform; and whether or not the group can influence the larger society. A sharing of values involves the fulfillment of the individual's values by the community, with a shared history

---

[49] Hirsch, Social Networks.

[50] Barry Wellman, Peter Carrington, and Alan Hall, "Networks as Personal Communities," in Social Structures: A Network Approach, eds. Barry Wellman and S. D. Berkowitz (Cambridge: Cambridge University Press, 1988), 130-184.

[51] Unger et al.

[52] Rook, 240.

[53] Unger et al.

[54] Unger et al.

and emotional connection."[55]

> Sharing life's more meaningful moments, its suffering and struggles, its triumphs and elation, constitutes the bond of friendship. Friends develop a sense of communion when they pursue a common interest, and when they cooperate and share responsibilities in a project . . ."[56]

While narrow in her understanding of persons who develop a sense of communion; that is limiting it to friends, Polcino supports the understanding that to maintain a sense of community, a shared history or bond must be present. We share some aspects of our identity with all our fellow human beings, other aspects with all Christians, and in particular the participants in this study share aspects of their identity as women religious.

> Erikson tells us that all persons are in a lifelong developmental movement from "I" to "we".[57] "We are always in search of a community that can offer us a sense of belonging . . ."[58] This may only contribute to a sense of well being, when the support given is offered within a relationship that is characterized by mutuality.[59] People have the need to feel that they are important in the life of the other. Rook has found that social exchanges with women that are imbalanced in either direction, receiving too much or too little, are associated with loneliness. It was found in a study by Williams et al. that loneliness was not affected by the number of persons listed as best friends for either the lonely or non-lonely, but rather it was the lack of intimacy perceived by the person listed as a best friend.[60] Results of a study by Rokach suggest that the loss of an important person or relationship, as well as an inadequate or crippled social support system, are the most common causes of loneliness.[61] This is

[55] Ibid. 155.
[56] Anna Polcino, Loneliness: The Genesis of Solitude, Friendship, and Contemplation, (Whitinsville: Affirmation Press, 1979), 7.
[57] Mofett.
[58] Henry Nouwen, Reaching Out: The Three Movements of the Spiritual Life, (Garden City: Doubleday & Company, Inc., 1978), 33.
[59] Rook.
[60] Williams et al.
[61] Rokach, "Antecedents."

supported by Mellor & Edelman.[62]   They report that the fewer number of confidants in a social network, the greater the loneliness.   This may generate a feeling of non-belonging or not being connected to others, or being rootless.

As well as being a part of a personal community through a variety of relationships; i.e., family, friend, co-worker, the individual is also linked to society through collectivities, such as the church, schools, and membership in organizations.   These "collectivities are based on the shared interest, personal affinities, or ascribed status of members who participate regularly in collective activities.   At the same time, the particular patterning of an individual's affiliations . . . defines his or her points of reference and determines his or her individuality."[63]   Membership in a collective brings with it patterns of behavior that demonstrate various types of interactions. When speaking of the Church collective, Garret refers to three interaction sequences: (a) a role reciprocity entered into between the person and his/her local church, (b) an interaction linking a believer and deity, and (c) ongoing relationships integrating the person into the official model of religion.[64]   The central teachings of the group relative to healthy faith and practice are assimilated into the personality and religious world view of the individual.   "Immured within this material appropriated by the self stand those normative role prescriptions that constitute spiritual health."[65]

Coetzee, in his study of the manifestation of religious commitment, states that common belief, acceptance of a common normative structure, and participation in a common ideal are some aspects which lead to social cohesion.[66]   Solidarity is found in the willingness to act together for the sake of common goals.   This feeling of belonging is based on an

[62] Karen Mellor and Robert Edelman, "Mobility, Social Support, Lonelines and Well-Being Amongst Two Groups of Older Adults," Personality and Individual Differences 9 (1988): 1-5.

[63] Ronald Breiger, "The Duality of Persons and Groups," in Social Structures: A Network Approach, eds. Barry Wellman and S.D. Berkowitz (Cambridge: Cambridge University Press, 1988), 84.

[64] William Garret, "Reference Groups and Role Strains Related to Spiritual Well-Being," in Spiritual well-being: Sociological Perspectives, ed. David Moberg (Washington, D.C.: University Press, 1979), 73-89.

[65] Ibid., 77.

[66] Jan Coetzee, "The Manifestation of Religous Commitment with Regard to Divergent Reality Definitions," in Spiritual Well-Being: Sociological Perspectives, ed. David Moberg (Washington, D.C.: University Press, 1979), 291-300.

experience of strong involvement in and loyalty to the church,[67] and rests to a great extent on identification with the church. When the church no longer figures into the world view of the member, the church ceases to figure into the life of the member and no longer contributes to spiritual well-being. Just as individual members of the church must be accountable to their commitment to the Church, so too the Church must be held accountable. "Loyalty and devotion to greater unity have a better opportunity of existing where corporate witness and symbolism are bound to establish a common bond."[68]

This common bond and sense of belonging to a community, in this case the Church, or the lack of it has a profound impact in the life of any person. This may be positive or negative. It has already been stated that loneliness is one of the consequences of a deficient social network and vice versa. The consequences do not stop there. They impact upon one's sense of spiritual well-being as well.

Spiritual Well-Being

As one speaks of the Church, one can readily see that "religion is not and cannot become a private matter".[69]

The subjective, personal religious experience, that is, the comprehension of that which can give one's life an absolute and unifying purpose, compels the person toward specific social conduct which objectifies his/her faith experience. Thus religion becomes a social reality which the person takes seriously in his social, political, and moral actions because they are given a   meaningful arrangement that can deliver him from his evil situation.[70]

It has been shown that one's social network system, in particular

---

[67] Ibid.; Patrick McNamara and Arthur St. George, "Measures of Religiosity and the Quality of Life: A Critical Analysis," in <u>Spiritual Well-Being: Sociological Perspectives</u>, ed. David Moberg (Washington, D.C.: University Press, 1979), 229-236.

[68] Coetzee, 297.

[69] Demosthenes Savramis, "Religion as Subjective Experience and Social Reality," in <u>Spiritual Well-Being: Sociological Perspectives</u>, ed. David Moberg (Washington D.C.: University Press, 1979), 119-131.

[70] Ibid., 128.

social/communal support, plays an important role in a person's sense of health and well-being both spiritual and psychological.[71] The concept of spiritual well-being consists of a meaningful, purposeful relationship with God through others, and is largely connected with the adequacy of one's social relationships.[72] Hungelmann et al. report in their study on spiritual well-being in older adults, that the need for "mutual loving, giving, and forgiving" is vital, resulting in harmony and interconnectedness."[73]

> "Its [spiritual well-being] functional definition pertains to the wellness or 'health' of the totality of the inner resources of people, the ultimate concerns around which all other values are focused, the central philosophy of life that guides conduct, and the meaning-giving center of human life which influences all individual and social behavior."[74]

Hateley cites Strommen in telling us that most psychologists treat religion as a topic to be avoided even though most Americans view it as important.[75] This is changing, however. Many authors are looking into spiritual well-being as an aspect of human life that is vital to our existence. The predominant perspective from these authors is that mental health is closely related to spiritual well-being, and there is no significant distinction between them.[76]

Moberg has been developing a theoretical and empirical program of analysis with regard to spiritual well-being, and feels that sociologists and psychologists need to investigate this vitally important phenomenon. Ellison conceptualizes spiritual well-being from two dimensions, vertical and horizontal. The vertical dimension, or religious well-being, refers to our

[71]Heller et al.; Wellman, Applying Network Analysis; Unger et al.; Rook.
[72] Arden Barden, "Toward New Directions for Ministry in Aging: An Overview of Issues and Concepts," Journal of Religion and Aging 1-2 (1986): 137-149; Verna Carson, Karen Soeken, Patricia Grimm, "Hope and its Relationship to Spiritual Well-Being," Journal of Psychology and Theology, 16 (1988): 159-167; Regina Marcum, "Religious Women's Communities and Spiritual Well-Being," in Spiritual Well-Being: Sociological Perspectives, ed. David Moberg (Washington, D.C.: University Press, 1979), 265-279; Moberg; Ellison; JoAnn Hungelmann, Eileen Kenkel-Rossi, Loretta Klassen, and Ruth Stollenwerk, "Spiritual Well-Being in Older Adults'" Journal of Religious and Health, 24 (1990):147-153.
[73] Ibid., 151.
[74] B. Hateley, "Spiritual Well-Being Through Life Histories," Journal of Religion and Aging 1 (1985): 2
[75] Ibid.
[76] Moberg.

sense of well-being in relation to God, and the horizontal dimension, or existential well-being, refers to a sense of life purpose and life satisfaction, with no reference to anything particularly religious.[77]   Paloutzian and Ellison adopted the definition used by the National Interfaith Coalition of Aging (1975). They define spiritual well-being as "the affirmation of life in relationship with God, self, community and environment that nurtures and celebrates wholeness."[78]

Carson et al. cite four characteristics of spiritual well-being that can be inferred from the above definitions given. They are as follows: 1. A unifying force that serves to integrate physical, mental, emotional and social dimensions of health; 2. Meaning in life which may serve as an inner drive for personal accomplishments; 3. A common bond between individuals which allows the sharing of warmth, love and compassion, a commitment to God . . .; and 4. Individual perceptions of faith that allows the individual to acknowledge the supernatural and to experience pleasure.[79]

> In one quite profound sense, definitions of spiritual well-being are always in the process of becoming. Just as the meaning of revelation and theological formulations persist as penultimate statements ever subject to revision and renewal, so too must notions of spiritual health endure as provisional standards to be reevaluated and reaffirmed by each new generation. What does remain constant, however, are the social processes by which a negotiated formula achieves formal status as the accepted definition . . . .[80]

The level of spiritual well-being in a person reflects the person's capacity to find purpose and meaning beyond one's self, in one's immediate situation, and in one's relationship to God. Religious belief can be a most powerful influence in one's life. Its effect can include changes in subjective experience and social behavior and supply purpose and meaning in life.[81]

When the purpose and meaning in life is deficient, one experiences a spiritual loneliness. It is a much more complex dimension of loneliness.

---

[77] Ellison.
[78] Ellison, 331.
[79] Carson et al.
[80] Garret, 89.
[81] Victor Frankl, The Unconscious God, (New York: Simon and Schuster, 1975).

"It designates various perceptions of the self. First, it designates the individual's relatedness to nature or the cosmos; secondly, it designates a sense of relatedness to God or a supreme being; and thirdly, it designates a sense of relatedness to what the person believes to be his or her unique destiny in life."[82] It is the latter two of these perceptions that will be used in this study. In spiritual loneliness, the person experiences him/herself as being out of touch with an ultimate source of life and meaning,[83] which results in feelings of emptiness and isolation.[84] Moustakas tells us that this type of loneliness is inescapable. It is a loneliness that is often marked with pain and suffering. It is through this that the seeds of new life grow. One must accept it, face it, and understand it if we are to live creative lives.[85] "It is here that we come to touch the life that connects us with ourselves, others, and with God."[86]

Dufton and Perlman tell us that some religious writers have described their faith as an effective deterrent against loneliness.[87] In fact, there is found to be a significant relationship between spiritual well-being and loneliness.[88] The higher one's level of spiritual well-being, the lower one's level of loneliness. Paloutzian et al. have reported that some forms of religiosity are more effective buffers against loneliness than others. They studied two issues; first, the study sought to show a relationship between loneliness and religiosity; and second, it sought to determine possible sources of such a relationship.[89] The study showed that the quality and quantity of people's relationships are among the strongest correlates of loneliness. It was also found that religious people have been found to employ specifically religious strategies to cope with loneliness, but the three groups, conservative religious, non-conservative religious, and non-religious did not differ on their measure of loneliness. Paloutzian et al. reasoned that

"there are different types of religious commitments that may be differentially related to quality of life and loneliness . . . those whose

[82] Rokach, "Theoretical Approaches," 236.
[83] Bosaint.
[84] Rokach, "Theoretical Approaches."
[85] Moustakas.
[86] Kelley Kelsey, "The Gift of Loneliness, Spirituality Today 36 (1984): 103.
[87] Brian Dufton and Daniel Perlman, "Loneliness and Religiosity: In the World But Not of it", The Journal of Psychology and Theology 14 (1986): 135-145.
[88] Ellison.
[89] Paloutzian et al.

religious commitment is very personal and intimate should have a greater sense of purpose in life, sense of belonging, satisfaction with existence, and less loneliness. Those who were non-religious were significantly more likely to feel a lack of companionship, not feel close to anyone, not have a sense of belonging, unable to reach out, and to feel totally alone."[90]

Spiritual well-being, religious and existential, are an important aspect of our sense of well-being and need to be considered when looking at not only spiritual well-being but psychological well-being as well. It is related to loneliness and social support. It lessens the degree of loneliness and increases the level of social support.

Community life

Understanding that loneliness, social/communal support, and spiritual well-being are closely interconnected, this study moves to look at a particular social network of persons, women in religious congregations, in relationship to these phenomena. Religious congregations of women are a particular type of church collective that have as a major part of their existence living communally. This demonstrates the intrinsic inseparability of the individual and social dimensions of the human person.[91] Religious congregations are social and religious entities that vary in the understanding of their mission, life style, prayer life, and charism, etc. Over time they have had periods of prosperity in numbers and at other times members have been scarce, as is the case today.[92] All would have their own rich history and traditions, and at the same time, all are linked through the common beliefs and traditions of the Roman Catholic Church.

This rich history and tradition of each congregation became a very vital part of the renewal that took place at the time of the second Vatican Council. In the early sixties, religious congregations throughout the world were mandated to renew their religious congregations. The how, the why, and the what were addressed in the Vatican Document Perfectae

---

[90] Ibid., 233.
[91] J. Sheets, "The Consecrated Life, Communio 9 (1982): 3-15.
[92] Lawrence Cada, Shaping the Coming Age of Religious Life (New York:Seabury Press, 1979).

Caritatis.[93] This was a document that was forever to alter religious life as it was known then into a continuing evolution today. While this study is only looking at community life in a limited fashion, the Vatican Council was to impact every facet of religious life. Religious life as it was known in the past is gone.[94]

Over the centuries religious congregations tended to move away from the original charism and mission of their original founders. Religious life became very structured and rigid. Leadership was authoritarian and hierarchical, with great emphasis upon absolute obedience to God through the superior. The rules and the customs were strictly adhered to and, in the process, the original intent or vision was often lost and the rules and customs themselves became important for their own sake.   It was mandated by Rome that each group again rediscover their beginnings and be willing to make changes in accord with their founding mission and charism. This brought about many changes, and with it, the fears and the tensions that can result when changes occur, often radical changes. Religious life was thrown into a state of confusion and pain. "Religious who were caught up between the old and the new, experienced confusion, turmoil, and a sense of loss, feeling cut off from traditional values and traditions".[95]   The authoritarian and hierarchical model of community life began to crumble, with a movement toward collegial models of living together. Women began to have a choice in what happened in their day-to-day living. What happened in a living community and the work place was no longer mandated. Choosing where one lived and worked became a possibility.   For many this was greatly welcomed, and for many it was painful and caused a great deal of resistance. The ability to make decisions for oneself was often a foreign experience for women religious.

> The very fact that religious don't have to live together as they once did now forces one to choose to be with others, to state publicly one's desire to be with a particular group, to own the need that they be "community" and that one is willing to sacrifice for that.[96]

---

[93] Vatican II: The Conciliar and Post Conciliar Documents, ed. Austin Flannery, O.P., Perfectae Caritatis (New York: Costello Publishing Company, 1975) 611-624.

[94] Donna Markham, "Communal Life and Global Reality" Human Development 8 (1987): 14-19.

[95] Mary Elizabeth Kenel, "Community: Problems of Loneliness and Ambivalence," Review for Religious 42 (1983): 715.

[96] Ibid., 721.

Emphasis on the individual surfaced.   The conflict between individualism and community life emerged. A movement away from looking at each individual as one in common with others without the recognition of individual differences began. This shift, for many, conveyed a sense of impermanence and fear of collapse. In the midst of this turmoil, one was able to begin cultivating her own gifts and talents, recognizing that this can only enrich the life of the community.[97]   At times, however, in the midst of the changes, the emphasis was placed on the individual to the detriment to community life. The intrinsic inseparability of the individual and social dimensions of the human person, however, has led women religious to find a balance of both dimensions. "The greater freedom allotted to individuals and local communities, the reinterpretation of the fundamental law as a description of vocation and spirit, and the relative absence of disciplinary norms have all placed a greater burden of responsibility on local communities and their members."[98] It is important to note, however, that not all communities have made these changes. There are still congregations who function with the old hierarchical model of governance with little ability for individuals to make choices for themselves.

Community is for all groups the process of becoming united through the common experience of a core vision.[99]   For many, this bond has a heavy emphasis on loving and mutually-satisfying relationships, characterized by exchange.   "Mutuality is the capacity to receive with respect and understanding the reality of another, and to offer to the other or others our own reality."[100] "In this process, we build structures that nurture our attention to the vision, and we seek ways of protecting the values inherent in the vision."[101]

What constitutes this sense of belonging or bondedness in religious communities? In Marcum's study of religious communities of women, the following consistently surfaced as important factors: (a) being person-oriented, (b) working and sharing together, (c) dependence on others, (d) prayer in spiritual life, and (e) quality of religious community life.[102]

---

[97] John Lozano, "Trends in Religious Life Today," Review for Religious 42 (1983): 481-503.
[98] Sheets, 491.
[99] Woodward.
[100] Ibid., 56.
[101] Ibid., 49.
[102] Marcum.

Aschenbrenner also places heavy emphasis on the above factors as well, and feels that it is a mandate for religious celibates to be effective and attractive in the Church today.[103]

While the community is a source for intimate and supporting friendships, Kenel tells us that a community member cannot expect community to be the sole source for relationships, and the meeting of our needs.[104] These require the presence of relationships outside the community membership. "Recognizing this will lead to a reduction in the unrealistic expectations that lead to frustration, anger, and disillusionment when the local community fails to meet these needs."[105] A delicate and decisive balance is needed between three essential relationships: a distinctive relationship with God, a life and faith shared in religious community, and a ministry shared with many other people.[106]

Belonging and identification call forth behaviors that are consistent with the goals of the group. When conflicts occur and the individual does not feel a sense of belonging, two aspects emerge; loneliness and a conflict between "individualism and community."[107] As a result self alienation, isolation, and marginality can be a part of an individual's experience while living in community, resulting in loneliness.

Like other segments of society, religious try to avoid the experience of loneliness in a variety of ways; i.e., overly dependent relationships, excessive work habits, excessive togetherness,[108] and at times an increased absence from the community.[109] This social isolation might engender feelings of rejection and disapproval by other members of the community.[110] Friendships within one's religious community as well as outside the community can alleviate some of the deepest roots of

---

[103] George Aschenbrenner, "Celibacy in Community and Ministry," Human Development 6 (1985): 27-33.

[104] Kenel.

[105] Ibid., 718.

[106] George Aschenbrenner, "A Celibate's Relationship with God," Human Development 5 (1984): 38-43.

[107] Kenel, 714.

[108] Bonsaint.

[109] Kenel.

[110] Ibid.

loneliness.[111] Just as one looks at social support from both positive and negative points of view, so one must look at religious life in the same way. "To assume in advance that 'community' will be all good, will be love and ecstasy, is to burden the experience with more than it can bear. Seeking only a community of love dooms the search."[112]

In summary, religious congregations of women are a particular type of social network where belonging and identification are vital. Meaning in life comes from a sense of commitment to God and those with whom they live and work. Spiritual well-being and social/communal support are vital and impact on the experience of loneliness within the individual. It is important to understand these concepts and how they affect women religious and ultimately their entire congregation. Healthy individuals will lead to healthy congregations.

[111] F. Omodio, "Loneliness and Friendship in Religious Life, Sisters Today 58 (1986): 160-163.
[112] Ralph Keyes, We, the Lonely People, (New York: Harper & Row, 1973), 162.

CHAPTER TWO

DESIGNING A BASIS FOR VIEWING
THE INSTRUMENTS NEEDED FOR WEAVING

Subjects

The subjects for this study were derived from fourteen religious congregations of women that have either a motherhouse or provincial house in the Archdiocese of Boston. Participants were sought only from those congregations where the major superior had granted permission for their membership to take part in the study. Thus, the study included the following congregations: Franciscan Sisters Immaculate Conception, OSF; Sisters of Notre Dame de Namur, SND (Ipswich Province); Poor Clare Nuns (Order of St Clare - Franciscan Sisters), OSC; Poor Clare Nuns (Order of St Clare), OSC; School Sisters of Notre Dame, SSND; Sisters of Charity (Halifax), SCH; Sisters of Montreal "Grey Nuns", SGM; Sisters of Charity at Ottawa, SCO; Sisters of Divine Providence, DP; Sisters of Jesus Crucified, CJC; Sisters of Providence, SP; Sisters of St Joseph (Boston), CSJ; Sisters of the Good Shepherd, RGS (active); Sisters of the Good Shepherd, RGS (contemplative). A stratified random sample was established by using groups that met the following criteria: active congregations with membership over one hundred; active congregations with membership under one hundred; and contemplative congregations. Using this criteria, the sample size from each congregation was determined by the percentage of each group in relationship to the total population within the group to which they belonged. 492 letters were sent out with 287 returning the questionnaires.

Each of the subjects in this study were given the following instruments to complete: The UCLA Loneliness Scale (Version 3), the Spiritual Well-Being Scale, and a Social Network List. They were also given a demographic sheet to fill out that gave access to background information; i.e., age, years in religious life, ministry, including retrospective data gathered for the time period 1960 - 1991. For each place of residence during that time period, each person ranked her experience of loneliness, spiritual well-being, and communal support on a scale of one to five, indicated the leadership style, and indicated whether she was there by choice or assignment.

INSTRUMENTS

The UCLA Loneliness (Version 3)

The UCLA Loneliness Scale (Version 3) was used. This measure is one that has had extensive use in the study of loneliness. The UCLA Loneliness Scale has come to be known as the "standard" scale in this area.[1] The first version of the scale had several difficulties. All the items were worded negatively, and issues of discriminant validity surfaced due to high correlations between loneliness and measures such as depression and self-esteem. The second version or the Revised version altered the scale having half of the statements with positive wording and half with negative wording. The internal consistency of the revised measure was high (coefficient alpha of .94) and compared favorably with alpha coefficient of .96 obtained in the original scale. The relationship between scores on the revised scale and measures of social activities and relationships were examined as a test of concurrent validity. This was done by finding a significantly high correlation with scores on the loneliness scale and other indicators of loneliness, social relationships, and affective states. Loneliness scores were also found not to be confounded by social desirability. The results demonstrated that the new measure was valid by the finding that lonely people report experiencing feelings of loneliness and do not report feelings unrelated to loneliness.[2]

A great deal of the early research with the loneliness scales was done using a college population, and more recently groups such as middle aged and elderly adults have been used. A problem that emerged in using the earlier scales with these groups was the complexity of the items. The words were difficult for some respondents to understand. As a result, the reliability and validity of the measure suffered.[3] A simplified version of the scale was devised. This scale consists of 20 items with 11 negatively-worded items and 9 positively-worded items. Each person is asked to respond to each statement on a 4 point Likert scale ranging from (1) never, to (4) always. The scores are tallied and the higher the score the lonelier

---

[1] Dan Russell and Carolyn Cutrona. (1990). <u>Development and Evolution of the UCLA Loneliness Scale</u> (Grants RO1-AG03846 & PO1-AG07094 from the National Institute of Aging) Iowa: University of Iowa, Center for Health Services Research, College of Medicine.
[2] Russell et al., "The revised UCLA Loneliness Scale."
[3] Russell et al., <u>Evolution</u>.

the subject. Scores can range from 20 - 80.

This new version has been used with a number of populations including college students, elderly, teachers, and nurses.[4] It appears to be very reliable with a coefficient alpha ranging from .89 to .94 across samples. A test-retest correlation of .73 was found in a sample of elderly persons over a period of 12 months. These results appear to be very similar to the results in earlier versions.[5] In a study by Russell et al., 489 college students were given several measures of loneliness and social support, as well as measures of related constructs, such as depression and social desirability. This simplified version was found to be significantly related to the scores on the NYU Loneliness Scale (r =.65) and the Differential Loneliness Scale (r =.72). Loneliness was, as expected, negatively associated with social support (r=.72).[6]

An extensive survey was done with 494 undergraduate and graduate students at the University of Iowa to determine whether Weiss's conceptualization of social and emotional loneliness can be distinguished as two separate forms of loneliness and whether or not they differ in the subjective experiences associated with them.[7] To measure these forms two different scales were used. The correlations with social and emotional loneliness were significantly different. Social loneliness was more strongly associated than emotional loneliness with not "feeling in tune with other people, not feeling a part of the group of friends, and not having a lot in common with other people."[8] Emotional loneliness was more closely related to feeling neither known nor close to anyone. When given the Revised UCLA Loneliness Scale, no differences were found between social and emotional loneliness on the Revised UCLA Loneliness Scale. Ninety-three percent of the correlations between social and emotional loneliness and the individual loneliness scale items were statistically significant at the .01 level. This suggests that the two forms of loneliness share a sizeably common core experience.

[4] Ibid.

[5] Ibid.

[6]Dan Russell, Elizabeth Altmaier, and Dawn Van Velzen, "Job Related Stress, Social Support, and Burnout Among Classroom Teachers," The Journal of Applied Psychology 72 (1987): 269-274.

[7] Russell et al., "Social and Emotional Loneliness: An Examination of Weiss's Typology of Loneliness," Journal of Personality and Social Psychology 6 (1984): 1313-1321.

[8] Ibid., 1317.

The Spiritual Well-Being Scale

The Spiritual Well-being Scale (SWB) was developed and then revised by Paloutzian et al.[9]   The SWB consists of 20 items responded to on a seven point scale, ranging from strongly agree to strongly disagree. Ten of the items are designed to measure Religious Well-Being (RWB), and 10 are designed to measure Existential Well-Being (EWB). Those items which contain a reference to God are contained in the RWB subscale, and those that pertain to well-being and meaning and purpose in life are contained in the EWB subscale. The sum of the two scores provides the overall SWB score. Total scores for SWB can range from 20 - 120. The range for both the RWB and EWB is 10 - 60. On all three scores, the higher the score the greater the sense of reported well-being. A factor analysis of the 20 items using the Varimax-rotation on data obtained from 206 students at three religiously-oriented colleges was done.

The factors clustered together as expected. The first three eigenvalues were 7.136, 2.716, 0.859. The factors were retained. All religious items loaded on the RWB factor. The existential factors appeared to load on two subfactors, one connoting life direction and one related to life satisfaction. The correlation between the subscales has ranged from .62 ($p < .001$) in two experiments with the initial 15 item version of the scale to .32($p < .001$) for the revised scale. High correlations have also been found between SWB and RWB ($r = .90$) and EWB ($r = .59$).

Test-retest reliability coefficients obtained from 100 students at the University of Idaho were .93 (SWB), .87 (RWB), and .78 (EWB). This suggests that the SWB has high reliability and internal consistency. The item content suggests good face validity. Bufford, Paloutzian, and Ellison report their studies demonstrate that the Spiritual Well-Being Scale has good test-retest reliability.[10] With a sample of 100, Paloutzian et al. tested and retested in a week's time resulting in a reliability coefficient of .93 (SWB), .96 (RWB), .86 (EWB).[11]

Paloutzian et al. have used the revised SWB in a series of studies

---

[9] Paloutzian et al.
[10] Rodger Bufford, Raymond Paloutzian, and Craig Ellison, "Norms for the Spiritual Well-Being Scale", Western Baptist Seminary and The Alliance Theological Seminary. 1990.
[11] Paloutzian et al.

involving over 500 respondents, including men, women, housewives, college students, young adults, senior citizens, religious, and non-religious people. Self esteem and SWB are found to be positively correlated, r = .44 (p < .001). It was found that SWB and intrinsic religious orientation were highly correlated (r = .67), mostly due to the RWB scale (r = .79, p < .001). SWB and extrinsic religious orientation were less positively related (r = .26, p < .001). Ellison cites Ellison and Economos as demonstrating that there is a strong positive relationship between spiritual well-being and those religious beliefs and practices which focus on the affirmation and valuing of the believer, r[68] = .68, p .001, and that the average amount of time spent per daily devotion period was significantly related to overall spiritual well-being, r[68] = .33, p < .01. Spiritual well-being was also positively related to the grounding of one's own positive self-evaluation in God's acceptance, r[68] = .60, p .001. This held for both RWB and EWB. Those who have a more intimate and positive relationship with both God and their Church have higher spiritual well-being.[12]

SWB scores have also correlated with other theoretically related scales. They were all found to be negatively correlated with the UCLA Loneliness Scale, positively with the Purpose in Life Test, intrinsic religious orientation, and self esteem.

It is important to note that Ledbetter, Smith, Vosler-Hunter, and Fischer found, in their study exploring the research and clinical usefulness of the Spiritual Well-Being Scale, that with religious samples, the relationship of scores on the SWB Scale and other variables are underestimated.[13]

Social Network List

Modeled after Hirsch, Stokes, and Stokes and Levin, this study looked at social networks and social support through the use of a social network list.[14] The subject was asked to list, using initials to indicate each person, up to 15 people who were significant in a positive or negative way

---

[12] Ellison.

[13] Mark Ledbetter, Leslie Smith, Hunter Vosler, L. Wanda, and James Fischer, "An Evaluation of the Research and Clinical Usefulness of the Spiritual Well-Being Scale," Journal of Psychology and Theology 19 (1991): 49-55.

[14] Hirsch; Stokes; Joseph Stokes and Ira Levin, "Gender Differences in Predicting Loneliness from Social Network Characteristics'" Journal of Personality and Sociality 51 (1986): 1069-1074.

to the individual and with whom she had contact at least once in a two week period. This was done with the communal living group as well as the individual's personal network. This provided the following measures: total size of the networks, the number of people the subject reports as close relationships, the number of persons one can turn to in an emergency and the density of the networks reported, using the formula of Hirsch, Heller, and Mansbach.[15]

$$D = \frac{X}{N \times (N-1)}$$

While this instrument is designed to gather a form of demographic data, it has been shown that there is an important connection between these factors and one's social network, having a direct impact on the person maintaining a sense of health and well-being.[16] A study by Stokes attempted to predict satisfaction with social support from a variety of variables derived from the subject's social network.[17] The components looked at were the size of the network, the number of confidants in the network, the dominance of relatives in the network, and the density of the network. Both the number of confidants and network size had an impact on satisfaction of social support. An exploration of the relation of the social network variables and loneliness was also done. The UCLA Loneliness Scale was used. Social networks were predictive of self-reported loneliness. Of the social network variables, the density of the network showed the strongest and most consistent relations to loneliness, with denser networks associated with being less lonely. In these denser networks, members were interconnected and important to each other.

Statistical Technique

The statistical analysis for this study was threefold, using three different data bases. In each case loneliness was the dependent variable.

---

[15] Hirsch, "Psychological dimensions."; Heller et al.
[16] Heller et al.
[17] Stokes et al.

Using the scores of both the loneliness scale and the spiritual well-being scale as well as the data gathered from the personal and communal networks, a Pearson's r correlation coefficient at the .05 level of significance was calculated. The goal was to determine whether there was a statistically significant correlation between spiritual well-being, and social/communal support in relationship to loneliness. Spiritual well-being includes religious well-being and existential well-being. Social/communal support consists of size, density, reciprocity, and type of relationship; i.e., confidant and those to whom one can turn in an emergency.   A factor analysis with a varimax rotation was then performed to determine whether loneliness, spiritual well-being, and social/communal support have any shared common factors.[18]

Using demographic data including age, level of education, type of congregation, type of commitment, style of governance, number of sisters in present residence, and present ministry, a Pearson's r correlation coefficient was run to determine whether or not any significant relationship existed between this data in relationship to loneliness, spiritual well-being, and social/communal support.   A multiple regression analysis was performed to determine whether or not any of the demographic data factors were statistically significant predictors of loneliness, spiritual well-being, and communal support.[19]

In an attempt to study how loneliness, spiritual well-being, and social/communal support have been experienced from 1960-to the present, and whether or not the radical changes in religious life have affected these phenomena, the participants were asked to reflect back as far as 1960, listing each place of residence, type of leadership style, whether they were assigned to these houses or chose to live there, how long they resided there, and how many sisters lived with them in each residence. Along with these questions, they were asked to rate each place of residence according

---

[18] Jae-on Kim and Charles Mueller, Introduction to Factor Analysis: What it is and How to do it, (Beverly Hills: Sage Publications, 1978); L. Gay, Educational Research: Competencies for Analysis and Application, 3d., (Columbus: Merrill Publishing Company, 1987); John Roscoe, Fundamental Research Statistics for the Behavioral Sciences, (New York: Holt, Rinehart, and Winston, Inc., 1969); Fred   Kerlinger, Foundations of Behavioral Research, (New York: Holt, Rinehart, and Winston, Inc., 1973).

[19]Dennis Hinkle, William Wiersma, and Stephen Jurs, Applied Statistics for the Behavioral Sciences, 2d ed., (Boston: Houghton Mifflin Co., 1983); Chris Spatz and James Johnston, Basic Statistics: Tales of Distribution, 3d ed., (Monterey: Brooks/Cole Publishing Co., 1984); F. Kerlinger and E. Pedhezau, Multiple Regression in Behavioral Research, (New York: Holt, Rinehart, and Winston Co., 1973).

to the degree of loneliness, spiritual well-being, and social/communal support they experienced at that time. The data for this analysis were both nominal and ordinal in nature. The nominal data included the following: The method used in determining where they lived, i.e., (1) assigned, or (2) chosen; the type of leadership, i.e., (1) superior, (2) house council, or (3)collegial, the number of sisters in each house, and the time frame for each residence.   The ordinal data represent their ratings of support, loneliness and spiritual well-being on a scale of 1-5. Given that the data are nominal and ordinal, a chi-square test for k independent samples was run to "enable data which are inherently classifitory or in ranks to be examined for significance."[20] Using the criterion variables of support, spiritual well-being, and loneliness, levels of significance were calculated, and standard residuals were run to determine where within those variables the significance resides.

---

[20] Sidney Siegel, <u>Nonparametric statistics</u>, (New York: McGraw-Hill, Inc., 1956), 160.

Hypotheses Tested at $p < .05$

It was hypothesized that there would be a statistically significant relationship found between measures of loneliness and measures of spiritual well-being in women religious; a statistically significant relationship between measures of loneliness and measures of social support in women religious; and statistically significant relationship between measures of spiritual well-being and measures of social/communal support in women religious.

Those sisters that presently live in settings where the decision-making process is collegial, i.e., each member has a part to play in the decision making process, will differ significantly in the frequency of their ratings for levels of loneliness, spiritual well-being, and communal support than those who live in settings where decisions are made by a superior or house counsel.

Those sisters who choose their place of residence will differ significantly in the frequency of their ratings for levels of loneliness, spiritual well-being, and community support from those who are assigned to their place of residence.

There will be statistically significant differences in the frequency of their ratings of levels of loneliness, spiritual well-being, and social/communal support in the four designated time periods established in this study from 1960 - 1991.

Sisters who have a strong supportive social network both within the congregation and outside the congregation will have statistically significant differences in measures of loneliness, spiritual well-being, and communal support than those who have a strong supportive network in only one of these areas, or those who have little support in either one or both.

There will be significant underlying factors shared by loneliness, spiritual well-being, and communal support.

Limitations

There may be a degree of bias in this study given that the author is a member of a religious congregation. This fact has the potential to effect the analysis of the findings reported here.

The fact that this study focusses only on women religious limits our understanding of the impact these variables may have upon religious life as a whole, leaving the experience of men in religious congregations, and diocesan clergy unknown. It is also limited to a small geographical area, the Archdiocese of Boston, limiting the ability to generalize to other areas of the United States.

Social support in this study looks at a limited number of facets: size, density, and the type of relationship, i.e., confidants, and those who can be relied upon to help in an emergency. It is structural in its nature and leaves out many factors such as relationships that are neutral, frequency of contact, length of time known, etc. The complexities of human relationships are greater than the scope of this study.

While all subjects were given each instrument as an internal control, the fact that they were solely self report does not allow us to know clearly to what degree the persons filling out the surveys attempted to look good; i.e., not lonely, having a high sense of spiritual well-being and social support, or to present themselves in a negative light; i.e., very lonely, lacking a sense of spiritual well-being and social support.

This study only deals with a small facet of religious life, namely communal support. Aspects such as prayer life and the vows of poverty, chastity, and obedience have not been addressed. Therefore any conclusions of this study cannot be generalized to all aspects of religious life. It is not possible to tell to what degree, if at all, these unaddressed facets impact upon the phenomena being studied.

In asking the subjects to recall their experiences of loneliness, spiritual well-being, and communal support in past living situations, it is difficult to determine how accurate their self report might be since we have no direct way to measure it. Care must be taken in interpreting the results.

CHAPTER THREE

STATISTICAL FINDINGS

Demographics

Four hundred ninety two questionnaires were sent out, with a return rate of 79%. The returns were divided into three categories: those who returned completed questionnaires, those who chose not to participate but wrote letters stating their reasons for not doing so, and those who responded beyond a date that inhibited the use of their data in this study. two hundred eighty nine women completed the materials sent, 100 responded by letter, and two returned their questionnaires, but their data were not incorporated into this study because they were received after the analysis of the data was completed.

There were a variety of reasons why 100 women chose not to take part in the study but responded by letter. For many, ill health was the primary reason. In some instances health care workers wrote to this author on their behalf, and in other instances the person wrote herself, at times quite painstakingly. The illnesses included the following: Alzheimer's disease, stroke, blindness, recent surgeries, emotional difficulties, Chrone's disease, and severe arthritis. Illness of family members was included, with several caring full time for their parents or siblings.

Time appeared to be an issue. Many felt overloaded with work commitments, and the pressure of the deadline was difficult for them. Several sisters were on sabbatical and felt this would take away from their present experience. Several stated that they simply did not like filling out questionnaires.

There were those who felt that they never felt lonely, nor did they have a problem with Spiritual Well-Being or community support, and, therefore, saw no reason to complete the questionnaires. Others felt that it did not speak to their experience, especially in the sections pertaining to social networks, while others found that responding to the questionnaire surfaced too many difficult feelings about the past.

Lastly there was a group who felt unqualified to take part in this study, finding it too difficult to complete. The major problem seemed to be the difficulty of the social network section of the packet. This difficulty, stated clearly by some, was also apparent with some of those women who completed the questionnaires. As a result of stated difficulties, 25 of those participating in the study did not complete the matrices for the communal and personal networks. Of this group five did not complete the entire communal network section, and 15 did not complete the personal network section.

The 287 women religious who took part in this study represented 14 religious congregations of women. Each sister was placed in the group to which her congregation belonged: active congregations over one hundred members, under one hundred members, or contemplative. See table 3.1

Table 3.1.--Total Number by Congregation

Congregation	Total Number
Contemplative	6
Active Under 100	32
Active Over 100	249

The average age of the 287 women was 64.7 with the youngest being 29 and the oldest 93. Three sisters were under 35 years of age, 10 between 35-44, 43 between 45-54, 70 between 55-64, 110 between 65-75, and 49 older than 75 years of age.

The subjects represent a highly educated group of women, with 87% holding a bachelor's degree or higher. See table 3.2 and figure 3.1 for the numbers in each category. The ministry of these women is quite varied. See table 3.3. All are involved in human services in some capacity. Even those who have retired do volunteer work in many areas. Involvement in the field of education represents 46% of this population commensurate with the mission of many congregations to educate those in need. Those that fall in the category of miscellaneous represent areas of ministry such as free lance writing, persons on sabbatical, volunteer work, and caring for elderly parents.

While there is a wide range in age and other demographic data, they did not have a measurable effect upon the loneliness, Spiritual Well-Being, Existential Well-Being, and Religious Well-Being scores; nor did they have a measurable effect upon their respective social networks.

Table 3.2.-- Total Number by Level of Education

Highschool Graduate	14
Bachelor's Degree	83
Master's Degree	152
Doctorate	16
Other	22

Figure 3.1.-- Levels of Education

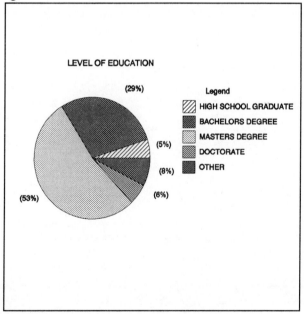

The mean scores and standard deviations for the variables of loneliness, Spiritual Well-Being and communal support can be seen in table 3.4. With

Table 3.3.--Total Number in Ministry

Ministry	Number
Education	131
Social Services	8
Pastoral Ministry	48
Community	32
Health Care	16
Counseling	6
Retired	18
Miscellaneous	27

Table 3.4.--Means and Standard Deviations

Column	Mean	SD
SWB	105.86	12.68
RWB	54.45	6.39
EWB	51.29	7.39
Loneliness	38.03	8.46

a potential score of 120 on the Spiritual Well-Being Scale, the mean score for Spiritual Well-Being was high with the mean score equal to 105.85. The highest score was 120 and the lowest score was 98. The higher the score on this scale the higher the person's level of Spiritual Well-Being. The potential score for religious wellbeing was 60 with a mean of 54.44. This is quite high. The highest score was 60 and the lowest score was 34.

The potential score for Existential Well-Being was 60 with a mean of 51.2. This too is quite high. The highest score was 60 and the lowest was 21. All three of these scaled scores are highly negatively skewed. See figure 3.2 for distribution of scores for Spiritual Well-Being. The distribution curves for Religious Well-Being and Existential Well-Being are similar. Scores on the UCLA Loneliness Scale can range from 20-80. The higher the score the higher is one's level of loneliness. The average score on this scale was 38.03. The highest was a score of 66 and the lowest a score of 20. The distribution of scores was positively skewed. See figure 3.3 for the distribution curve.

Figure 3.2.-- Distribution Curve for Spiritual Well-Being

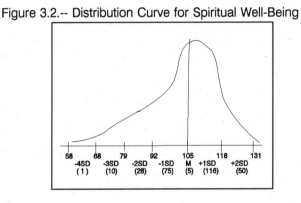

Figure 3.3.-- Distribution Curve for Loneliness Scores

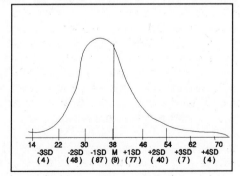

The total number in both the communal network and personal network ranged from 0-15 with 15 being the maximum possible number and an average in each network of 8.84 and 9.42 respectively. Each network was broken down into the following categories: confidants, those to whom one can turn in an emergency, those persons with whom one has a positive relationship, and those with whom they have a negative relationship. See their averages in table 3.5.

Table 3.5.-- Network Averages

	CN	PN
Confidants	3.0	3.7
Help/Emergency	5.6	6.3
Pos/Relationship	6.2	7.2
Neg/Relationship	1.1	0.7

* CN = Communal Network; PN = Personal Network

Demographics: Network Variables

Correlational studies and a multiple regression analysis was done to determine whether any aspect of the demographic data might be a predictor of loneliness, Spiritual Well-Being, and social support. See table 3.6 for correlation coefficients. In viewing the data, one can see that a strong correlation exists between loneliness and Spiritual Well-Being, but no correlations were found to exist between these phenomena and the demographics of age, level of education, type of community, ministry, socialization with co-workers or decision making style.

Similar tests were run using the demographic data and the communal and personal networks. The only demographic that had any significant effect upon the networks was that of age. A significant relationship exist between age and density of one's communal network with $r = -0.1849$. As one grows older, the communal network becomes less dense. A negative correlation exists between the number of persons with whom a positive significant relationship exists within the personal network and one's age is found, r = -0.2552. A negative correlation with the number of confidants

Table 3.6.-- Correlations of Demographic Data with Loneliness and SWB.

	age	educa	congre	minis	social	lone	swb
age	1.000	-0.0300	-0.0634	0.1424	-0.1801*	-0.1487	0.0894
educ		1.0000	-0.0500	0.0481	0.0632	-0.0273	-0.0376
congre			1.0000	-0.0438	0.0107	0.1386	-0.0380
ministry				1.0000	-0.2927*	0.0185	-0.0196
social					1.0000	0.0260	-0.0196
loneliness						1.0000	0.4035*
swb							1.0000

Note. *p < 0.05

within the personal network, r =-0.2486 was found as well. As one grows older the number of confidants and positive significant relationships within the personal network decreases. While age shows statistical significance in these areas, the multiple regression found that none of the demographics including age were predictors of communal support.

Correlations: Loneliness, Spiritual Well-Being and Communal and Personal Networks

The correlational study with loneliness as the dependent variable; Spiritual Well-Being (SWB), Existential Well-Being (EWB), Religious Well-Being (RWB), and communal support as independent variables has resulted in a number of statistically significant relationships. See tables 3.7 and 3.8. Loneliness was found to have a statistically significant negative correlation with Spiritual Well-Being, Religious Well-Being, and Existential Well-Being with r= -.4667, -.3511, and -.5009 respectively. When the level of loneliness is low, Spiritual Well-Being, Existential Well-Being, and Religious Well-Being scores are high, indicating a higher level of well-being. When

Well-Being scores are high, indicating a higher level of well-being. When the level of loneliness is high, the level of Spiritual Well-Being, Religious

Table 3.7.--Correlation Values for Communal Network.

	SWB	RWB	EWB	Helper	+Rel	-Rel	Loneliness
SWB	1.0000	0.9060*	0.9347*	0.1186	0.1017	-0.1014	-0.4667*
RWB		1.0000	0.7129*	0.0794	0.0714	-0.0508	-0.3511*
EWB			1.0000	0.1301	0.1037	-0.1256	-0.5000*
Help in Emergency				1.0000	0.7371*	-0.1074	-0.2260*
Positive Relationship					1.0000	0.0093	-0.1652
Negative Relationship						1.0000	0.2469*

Note. Abbreviations listed above for Spiritual Well-Being, Existential Well-Being, and Religious Well-Being will be used in any table of data. df = 286.
r > 0.1780. *p < 0.05

Table 3.8.--Correlation Values for Personal Network

	SWB	RWB	EWB	Helper	+Rel	-Rel	Loneliness
SWB	1.0000	0.9060*	0.9347*	0.1643	0.1134	-0.0418	-0.4667*
RWB		1.0000	0.7129*	0.1212	0.1116	-0.0044	-0.3511*
EWB			1.0000	0.1768*	0.1016	-0.0825	-0.5000*
Help in Emergency				1.0000	0.7885*	-0.0246	-0.2070*
Positive Relationship					1.0000	0.0224	-0.1617
Negative Relationship						1.0000	0.1991*

df = 286. r > 0.1780. *p < 0.05

Well-Being, and Existential Well-Being is low. The null hypothesis, that there would be no statistically significant relationship between loneliness and Spiritual Well-Being, Existential Well-Being, and Religious Well-Being in women who belong to religious congregations is rejected.

A number of statistically significant relationships were found to exist between loneliness and communal support. A "negative relationship" was found between loneliness and persons to whom one can turn in time of need with r=-.2070 in their personal network and r=-.2260 in their communal network. The larger the network of persons to whom one can turn in time of need, the lower the level of loneliness. The smaller this network, the higher one's level of loneliness. A "positive correlation" exists between loneliness and those significant others perceived to be a negative relationship with r=.2469 in communal support and r=.1991 for personal network and r=0.2469 in the communal network. Higher numbers of negative relationships appear to result in higher levels of loneliness. When looking at loneliness and communal support there is a significant correlation in their relationship. Loneliness is affected by the number of persons one can turn to in an emergency, and those who have significant others who have an impact on them in a negative way. While not all the factors of the given networks have a statistically significant relationship with loneliness, those that do enable one to reject the null hypothesis that there would be no statistically significant relationship between loneliness and communal support with the specific areas noted.

Using numbers as a way of representing strength within each network, the totals of each of the networks themselves and the total of both networks combined were calculated. Correlations between loneliness, Spiritual Well-Being, existental well-being, and Religious Well-Being were calculated. See table 3.9. It was hypothesized that there would be no statistically significant results when correlating the strength of the individual networks, as well as the strenth of the two networks combined with loneliness, Spiritual Well-Being, Religious Well-Being, and Existential Well-Being. This was found to be true with one exception. The number of negative relationships in the personal network and the combined total of both networks have a statistically significant relationship to loneliness with r = 0.1820. The more negative relationships within the personal network, the higher one's level of loneliness. This impacts therefore on the total number of negative relationships within both networks with resulting statistically significant findings with r = 0.1882.

It was also hypothesized that there would be no statistically significant relationship between Spiritual Well-Being and communal support in women belonging to religious congregations. This was proven to be true. A statistically significant correlation between Spiritual Well-Being and the variables for communal and personal networks was not found. When Spiritual Well-Being is treated by itself, however, one finds that it is highly correlated with Religious Well-Being and Existential Well-Being with r =.9060

Table 3.9.-- Correlations for Numbers in Networks and Loneliness, SWB, Support

	Loneliness	SWB	RWB	EWB
COMMUNAL NETWORK				
Help in an Emergency	-0.1533	0.1117	0.0894	0.1095
Positive Relationship	0.1092	-0.0944	0.0703	0.0933
Negative Relationship	0.1406	-0.0639	-0.0290	-0.0793
PERSONAL NETWORK				
Help in an Emergency	-0.0854	0.1801*	0.14995	0.1782*
Positive Relationship	-0.0524	0.1484	0.1484	0.1365
Negative Relationship	0.1820*	-0.0517	-0.0517	-0.1018
TOTAL OF BOTH NETWORKS				
Help in an Emergency	-0.1384	0.1742	0.1428	0.1718
Positive Relationship	-0.0948	0.1466	0.1275	0.1386
Negative Relationship	0.1882*	-0.0708	-0.0156	-0.1057

*$p < 0.05$. $r > 0.1780$

& $r = .9347$ respectively. When Spiritual Well-Being is high Religious Well-Being and Existential Well-Being are high. When Spiritual Well-Being is low Religious Well-Being and Existential Well-Being is low. Religious Well-Being and Existential Well-Being are also highly correlated with one another with $r = .7129$. The higher one's sense of Existential Well-Being the higher is one's Religious Well-Being and vice versa. See table 3.8.

Factor Analysis

A factor analysis with varimax rotation was performed with the variables of loneliness, Spiritual Well-Being, and social support (both communal and personal) to determine if there were significant underlying factors that all these variables share in common. In determining how many common factors were involved, if any, eigenvalues for both networks in relationship to loneliness (the dependent variable), and Spiritual Well-Being, Religious Well-Being, and Existential Well-Being (independent variables) were calculated. Only those eigenvalues with a value greater than one were retained. The computed eigenvalues show that there are three very strong factors for both networks. The eigenvalues for each network are listed in table 3.10.

Table 3.10.-- Communal And Personal Network Eigenvalues

Communal Network			
Loneliness With SWB	2.5776	1.5359	1.4537
Loneliness With RWB	2.5629	1.4818	1.3891
Loneliness With EWB	2.5771	1.5750	1.4591

Personal Social Network			
Loneliness With SWB	2.4639	1.5299	1.3857
Loneliness With RWB	2.4549	1.4892	1.2952
Loneliness With EWB	2.5771	1.5750	1.4591

Note. EIGENVALUES >1, *p < 0.05

When considering loneliness, Spiritual Well-Being, and Existential Well-Being in both networks, the following three factors were established: factor one represents a lack of engagement and connectedness; factor two represents a lack of meaning and purpose in life; and factor three represents a lack of cohesion and belonging. See table 3.11. When considering loneliness and Religious Well-Being in both networks, a shift in their meaning takes place. Factor one remains the same, the second factor, however, represents an isolation from self and other, and the third factor represents a lack of relatedness to God. See table 3.12.

Table 3.11.-- Factors

Loneliness - Spiritual Well-Being/Existential Well-Being

Factor One - A Lack of Engagement and Connectedness
Factor Two - A Lack of Meaning and Purpose in Life
Factor Three - A Lack of Cohesion and Belonging

Table 3.12.-- Factors

Loneliness - Religious Well-Being

Factor One - A Lack of Engagement and Connectedness
Factor Two - Isolation from Self and Other
Factor Three - A Lack of Relatedness to The Ultimate Other

The rotated factor loadings can be seen in table 3.13. The variables that loaded onto factor one, a lack of an engaging and connected social network, are those variables that address particular types of relationships, i.e., those who can be counted on to help in an emergency, those who are confidants, and those that have a positive significant relationship with the participant, along with the density of each network. When an engaging social network, represented by helper, positive significant other, and confidant in both networks is not present, the greater one's experience of non-connectedness leading to a greater experience of loneliness. The more dense the network, that is the larger the number of pairs within a network that relate to one another apart from the participant in this study, the greater the sense of non-connectedness which can also lead to a greater experience of loneliness.

Loneliness, Spiritual Well-Being and Existential Well-Being load onto factor two. The loneliness in this factor is largely connected to a spiritual loneliness which addresses meaning-making and at the same time is indirectly related to emotional loneliness that results in a loss of a significant other. The less meaning one finds in life the higher is one's level of loneliness and the lower one's level of Spiritual Well-Being and Existential Well-Being. The density of each network decreases as does the experience of loneliness. The only variables to load on more than one factor are density and significant negative relationships. Within the person's personal network density loads on factors 1 and 3. Within the communal network it loads onto all three factors. Significant negative relationships load onto factors 2 and 3.

Table 3.14 shows the factors when considering loneliness and Religious Well-Being. Factor one remains the same: the lack of an engaging

Table 3.13.-- Rotated Factor Loadings

		LEGEND		

PS = Personal Social Network
CS = Communal Social Network
H   = Help in an Emergency
+   = Positive Relationships
-   = Negative Relationships
CF = Confidant
DN = Density

Var	F1	F2	F3	Com	Var	F1	F2	F3	Com
Lone	.0504	.8383*	-.0613	.7091	Lone	.1370	.8188*	.0032	.6892
SWB	-.0912	-.7659*	.0799	.6012	SWB	-.0777	-.7727*	-.0077	.6032
HPS	-.8933*	-.1194	.1303	.8293	HCS	-.8625*	-.1151	.1451	.7782
+PS	-.8921*	-.0541	.0862	.8062	+CS	-.8264*	-.1393	.2037*	.7439
-PS	-.0203	.4347*	.4596*	.4006	-CS	-.1473	.3760*	.6912*	.6409
CFPS	-.7040*	-.0105	-.1524	.5190	CFCS	-.7433*	-.0655	.0480	.5591
DNPS	.3332*	-.1690	.7477*	.6986	DNCS	.5496*	-.3516*	.5197*	.6958

Var	F1	F2	F3	Com	Var	F1	F2	F3	Com
Lone	.0582	.8343*	-.0937	.7083	Lone	.1305	.8295*	-.0329	.7061
EWB	-.0813	-.7974*	.0714	.6476	EWB	-.0798	-.7966*	-.0241	.6415
HPS	-.8944*	-.1164	.1303	.8305	HCS	-.8639*	-.1091	.1380	.7772
+PS	-.8931*	-.0419	.0839	.8064	+CS	-.8283*	-.1400	.1970*	.7446
-PS	-.0187	.4605*	.4337*	.4005	-CS	-.1623	.4016*	.6638*	.6282
CFPS	-.7031*	-.0175	-.1523	.5178	CFCS	-.7433*	-.0539	.0443	.5573
DNPS	.3288*	-.1607	.7605*	.7123	DNCS	.5442*	-.3103*	.5506*	.6955

*$p < 0.05$

Table 3.14.--Rotated Factor Loadings

LEGEND

PS = Personal Social Network
CS = Communal Social Network
H = Help in an Emergency
+ = Positive Relationships
- = Negative Relationships
CF = Confidant
DN = Density

Var	F1	F2	F3	Com	Var	F1	F2	F3	Com
Lone	.0440	.0548	.8279*	.6903	Lone	.1595	-.0461	.7947*	.6591
RWB	-.1012	-.1076	-.6567*	.4531	RWB	-.0560	-.0127	-.6873*	.4757
HPS	-.8924*	-.1327	-.1103	.8262	HCS	-.8637*	-.1473	-.1114	.7801
+PS	-.8911*	-.0901	-.0630	.8062	+CS	-.8280*	-.2057*	-.1230	.7431
-PS	-.0268	-.4753*	.4650*	.4428	-PS	-.1270	-.7225*	.3536*	.6632
CFPS	-7030*	.1539	-.0225	.5184	CFCS	-.7450*	-.0460	-.0775	.5631
DNPS	.3403*	-.7364*	-.1732	.6881	DNCS	.5440*	-.4837*	-.4116*	.6994

*$p < 0.05$

and connected social network. The second factor represents isolation from self and others. The greater the sense of isolation the lower is one's sense of Existential Well-Being. In this factor, density with the social network is seen differently from the other two factors. Higher density is in this instance positively related to having meaning and purpose in life. The greater the meaning in one's life, the lower one's level of loneliness, and the higher one's level of Spiritual and Existential Well-Being. The third factor represents a lack of cohesion and belonging to a social network. If there is a strong sense of not belonging and a lack of cohesion, the number of negative significant relationships and the density of each network increases, resulting in a greater sense of loneliness. When a sense of cohesion and belonging is strong, the number of negative relationships and an increase in the density of the network leads to an increase of loneliness. The third factor is a lack of relatedness to God. When one experiences a lack of relatedness to the Ultimate Other, there are higher levels of loneliness with a decrease in Religious Well-Being. When one experiences relatedness to God, the Ultimate Other, there is less loneliness with a greater sense of Religious Well-Being. Again the only variables to load onto more than one factor are density and significant negative relationships. In the personal network, density loads onto factors one and two, with significant negative relationships loading onto factors two and three. In the communal network density loads on to all three factors, and significant negative relationships load onto two and three. Again density is indicative of less connectedness and a sense of isolation from self and other, but in the communal network the higher density represents greater Religious Well-Being and less lonelinss and a greater connnectedness to God, the Ultimate Other.

1960 to the Present

Data to this point have dealt with the present. A shift is now made in the discussion as one moves from the present to the past. The question asked is "how have the radical changes in religious life over the past three decades impacted upon women religious and their experience of loneliness, Spiritual Well-Being, and communal support"? A statistically significant relationship between loneliness, Spiritual Well-Being, and communal support over three decades is present. See table 3.15. There is a strong negative correlation between between loneliness and communal support, r = 0.4097, and loneliness and Spiritual Well-Being, r = -0.3232. A positive correlation

Table 3.15.-- Correlations of Data over time. 1960 - 1991

	#YRS	#SRS	CHOICE	SUPPORT	SWB	STYLE	LONE	TRANS.IY
#YRS	1.0000	0.0628	0.0716	0.1743	0.1898*	0.1464	-0.1323	0.0981
#SRS		1.0000	-0.1039	0.0344	0.0872	-0.2220*	0.0158	0.0807
CHOICE			1.0000	0.0462	0.0708	0.5486*	-0.0275	-0.6126*
SUPPORT				1.0000	0.6025*	0.1181	-0.4097*	-0.0760
SWB					1.0000	0.1175	-0.3232*	-0.1228
STYLE						1.0000	-0.0635	-0.4815*
LONE							1.0000	-0.0393
TRANS.IY								1.0000

Note. Transiy = year beginning each residence. *p < 0.05

exists among support with Spiritual Well-Being with $r = 0.6025$. Given these results, the null hypothesis that stated there would be no statistically significant relationships between these variables over the three decades is rejected.

Along with studying the relationship between loneliness, Spiritual Well-Being, and communal support, this study looked at the variables of method by which residence was determined, leadership style within this residence, and the entry year for each place of residence since 1960, the number of sisters with whom they reside, and the length of time in each residence. The length of residence in one place was found to be positively correlated with Spiritual Well-Being with $r = 0.1898$. The longer one resides in one place the higher is one's sense of Spiritual Well-Being. A chi-square test for k independent samples was done to determine whether or not the groups established by year, method of choice, and leadership style differed with respect to loneliness, Spiritual Well-Being, and support. This involved 1,437 discrete observations each giving the initial year, method of choice, leadership style, and levels of loneliness, Spiritual Well-Being, and communal support. There were four groupings by year, 1960-66, 1967-76, 1977-86, and 1987-1991. Two groups were established for method; assignment or choice, and three groups were established for leadership style; superior, house council, and collegial decision making. A significant relationship was to be found among method, year, and leadership style in relationship to Spiritual Well-Being and communal support, but there was no significant difference found when comparing loneliness to method, year, or leadership style. See table 3.16 for values of significance. Standard residuals were calculated to determine what cells were statistically significant. This was done by pairing the possible combination of variables; support and method of choice, support and leadership style, support and

Table 3.16.--Chi-Square levels of significance

Criterion Variables	Year	Method	Leadership
Support	46.713*	36.9617*	63.0171*
SWB	40.215*	28.2358*	38.5428*
Loneliness	11.143	7.095	13.5148

*$p < 0.05$

time period, spiritual well-being and method of choice, spiritual well-being and style of leadership, Spiritual Well-Being and time period. See table 3.17 for significnace between support and method of choice. Support ranged in values from 1 to 5 with one being very low to five being very high. Significance occured in three cells. Those who rated support 3 (average) and were assigned to their residence had significantly higher frequency of more persons at this level than statistically expected. Those who chose their place of residence had a significantly lower frequency than expected for those rating support at three. Those who chose their place of residence and rated their support as 5 (very high) had a significantly higher frequency than expected at this rating. Similar findings occur when viewing method of choice and Spiritual Well-Being. See table 3.18. Those sisters who rate their Spiritual Well-Being with a 3 (average) show a statistical significance in the frequencies in both categories, assigned and chosen. Those sisters who were assigned to their place of residence have significantly higher

Table 3.17.--Chi-Square for support vs Method

	Assigned	Chosen	Standard Residual
Support 1	O 28	34	A = 1.18
	E 35	27	C = 1.35
Support 2	O 83	70	A = 0.42
	E 87	66	C = 0.49
Support 3	O 305	149	A = 2.93*
	E 258	195	C = 3.29*
Support 4	O 266	221	A = 0.66
	E 277	209	C = 0.83
Support 5	O 129	138	A = 1.94
	E 153	115	C = 2.14*

Note. A = Assigned, C = Chosen, *p<0.05

Table 3.18.-- Chi-Square Spiritual Well-Being vs Method

		Assigned	Chosen	Standard Residual
SWB 1	O 15		14	A = 0.49
	E 35		27	C = 0.58
SWB 2	O	75	49	A = 0.47
	E 71		53	C = 0.55
SWB 3	O 346		192	A = 2.28*
	E 306		231	C = 2.56*
SWB 4	O 251		247	A = 1.90
	E 283		214	C = 2.26*
SWB 5	O 124		110	A = 1.90
	E 134		101	C = 2.26*

Note. A = Assigned, C = Chosen, *p<0.05

frequency of persons at this level than expected, and those who chose their place of residence show significantly less than expected. Sisters who rated their well being as a 4 (high) and chose their place of residence had significantly greater frequencies than expected.

Based on these findings, the null hypothesis that stated that there would be no significant difference in the frequencies of ratings for support and Spiritual Well-Being on any level for those who chose where they would live and those who were assigned is rejected only for those who rate their support as average or very high and those who rate their Spiritual Well-Being as average or high. The other levels show no statistical significance.

Similar results are also found in relationship to communal support and Spiritual Well-Being with leadership style within each residence. See Tables 3.19 and 3.20. Those sisters that rated the degree of support and

Table 3.19.-- Chi-Square of Support vs Leadership

	Superior	Council	Collegial	Standard Residual
Support 1	O 27	5	26	S = 1.41
	E 29	6	25	H/C = 0.58
				C = 0.41
Support 2	O 70	15	63	S = 0.12
	E 71	16	53	H/C = 0.25
				C = 0.26
Support 3	O 264	33	140	S = 3.72*
	E 306	47	231	H/C = 2.56*
				C = 3.11*
Support 4	O 195	72	206	S = 2.00*
	E 225	51	195	H/C = 2.26*
				C = 0.79
Support 5	O 100	25	137	S = 2.16*
	E 124	28	107	H/C = 0.39
				C = 2.90*

Note. S = Superior. H/C = House Council. C= Collegial. *$p < 0.05$

Spiritual Well-Being at 3 (average) show a statistically significant difference in the expected frequencies and leadership styles. In relationship to support, those residing in a residence that has had a superior have a higher than expected number of persons at this level. Those who have a house council or collegial leadership show a lower than expected frequency. In relationship to Spiritual Well-Being, those sisters that lived within a residence with a superior as leader had statistically higher frequency than expected and for collegial style significantly less than expected.

Those who report a rating of 4 (high) show significance in both superior and house council modes of leadership. Those with a superior are lower than expected in frequency and those with a house council had a higher than expected frequency. Those who rate support a 5 (very high) show a lower than expected frequency when superiors are found, and higher than expected frequency with those who live in a collegial setting. Those who rate their level of Spiritual Well-Being as a 4 (high) coupled with having a superior show that there were significantly less than the number expected. No other significance was found in relationship to leadership style and Spiritual Well-Being. The hypothesis that states there would not be statistically significant differences in the frequencies of one's level of support and Spiritual Well-Being and leadership styles is rejected only when rating each of these as 3(average) for both support and Spiritual Well-Being, when support is rated as 4(high) and 5(very high), and when Spiritual Well-Being is rated as 4(high).

It was hypothesized that the the levels of support in any of the time periods established from 1960 to the present would not show statistically significant differences in the ratings of 1 through 5, very low to very high. When viewing the phenomena of support over a period from 1960 to the present, we again see statistically significant results. See table 3.21. Those persons who rated their support at 3 (average) show significance when the time span covers 1987-1991. The number of persons in this category is significantly lower than the number expected. The time span from 1960-66 has more than is expected. Those who rate their support as 5 (very high) show a statistically significant difference in expected frequencies for 1987-91. The outcomes were higher than expected. The null hypothesis is rejected only for average and very high ratings of support within the time span from 1987-1991 with a higher than expected frequency.

There are also a number of significant results, see table 3.22, in relationship to Spiritual Well-Being and span of years. Again it was hypothesized that there would be no statistically significant differences in frequencies of the ratings for Spiritual Well-Being and the established time periods. This was found to be true except for the following: When rating Spiritual Well-Being at 3 (average), those sisters in 1987-91 and 1977-86, had significantly less frequency than expected, those who rated it a three from 1960-66, had a higher frequency than expected. Those who rated it at 5 (very high) in the time period from 1987-91 have a higher frequency of persons than expected. The null hypothesis is rejected only for those rating their level of spiritual well- being as average and very high with a larger than expected frequency at this level in relationship to assigned time spans.

Table 3.20.-- Chi-Square Leadership vs Spiritual Well-Being

	Superior	Council	Collegial	Standard Residual
SWB 1	O 17	1	10	S = 1.11
	E 13	3	12	H/C = 0.71
				C = 0.41
SWB 2	O 66	9	47	S = 1.19
	E 57	13	50	H/C = 1.11
				C = 0.42
SWB 3	O 285	54	178	S = 2.28*
	E 249	56	215	H/C = 0.27
				C = 2.52*
SWB 4	O 197	61	223	S = 2.18*
	E 230	52	199	H/C = 1.25
				C = 1.70
SWB 5	O 91	25	113	S = 0.71
	E 109	25	94	H/C = 0.00
				C = 1.96*

Note. S = Supreior. H/C = House Council. c = Collegial *p < 0.05

Table 3.21.-- Chi-Square support vs year

		1987-91	1977-86	1967-76	1960-66	Standard Residual
Support 1	O	3	18	29	12	1.22 (1)
	E	6	13	24	18	1.39 (2)
						1.02 (3)
						1.41 (4)
Support 2	O	16	33	65	39	0.53 (1)
	E	14	33	60	46	0.00 (2)
						0.65 (3)
						1.03 (4)
Support 3	O	23	79	173	179	2.93*(1)
	E	42	98	179	135	1.91 (2)
						0.45 (3)
						3.78*(4)
Support 4	O	54	109	198	126	1.34 (1)
	E	45	105	192	145	0.39 (2)
						0.43 (3)
						1.58 (4)
Support 5	O	35	67	97	69	2.00*(1)
	E	25	58	106	80	1.18 (2)
						0.87 (3)
						1.23 (4)

1 = 1987-91. 2 = 1977-86. 3 = 1967-76. 4 = 1960-66. $*p < 0.05$

Table 3.22--Chi-Square Spiritual Well-Being vs Year

	1987-91	1977-86	1967-76	1960-66	Standard Residual
SWB 1 O 2	8	11	8	0.58 (1)
E 3	6	11	9	1.41 (2)
				0.00 (3) 0.33 (4)
SWB 2 O 10	24	54	36	0.30 (1)
E 11	27	49	37	0.58 (2)
				0.71 (3) 0.16 (4)
SWB 3 O 31	93	222	192	2.69*(1)
E 50	116	212	160	2.14*(2)
				0.69 (3) 2.53*(4)
SWB 4 O 55	119	198	126	1.33 (1)
E 46	107	196	148	1.16 (2)
				0.14 (3) 1.81 (4)
SWB 5 O 34	63	77	61	2.55*(1)
E 22	51	93	70	1.68 (2) 1.66 (3) 1.07 (4)

*$p < 0.05$

Openended Question

Sixty three sisters responded to the open ended question on whether or not they felt there was anything else that they found important to say about loneliness, Spiritual Well-Being, and communal support. A number of issues were raised around these phenomena, especially in regard to loneliness. Loss was a recurrent theme whether coming from death of family members or friends, illness in self or others, uprooting from one living setting to another. All have had a marked impact on their level of loneliness. A sense of loneliness was also felt in large institutional settings, being away at school or the missions. The time of Vatican II was a time of turmoil and for some a very lonely and isolating time with little communal support from others.   This loneliness for many is countered by good communal networks, family and personal ties, or the development of authentic community. There are of course those who state they have never been lonely in their life time.

This text now moves from the presentation of the results to analysis of the data. This offers the opportunity to reflect on its implications for women belonging to religious congregations.

CHAPTER FOUR

DEVELOPMENT OF THE WOVEN CLOTH: A NEW PARADIGM

Loneliness and Spiritual Well-Being

The response rate for this study resulted in a 79% return rate. While 14 congregations are represented in this study, one must keep in mind that many of the congregations were quite small. Using a stratified random sample helped in allowing more persons from these smaller congregations to be a part of the study. Even given this fact, the greater numbers are from those active congregations having more than 100 members, with the Sisters of St. Joseph having the highest number of participants. This is fitting in that they are indeed the largest congregation within the Archdiocese of Boston. The number of contemplative congregations represented were very small resulting in only having 6 sisters taking active part in the study. There were no statistically significant findings when looking at the different representative groups of active and contemplative congregations.

Loneliness as measured on the UCLA Loneliness Scale (Version 3) speaks to the absence or deficiency of relationships in the present.[1] The types of deficiency can be varied depending on how a person sees and experiences one's own from others.[2] It may mean a lack of an intimate other and/or a lack of a network to which one belongs.[3] Varied deficiencies can be seen in the following responses given by participants in this study: "In a large house situation a person can become very lonely - they can be lost in the struggle", "the years . . . lived in Africa where loneliness was a part of life 8,000 miles away from things familiar", "When death came to me in the person of my mother, father, and nephew, I was alone without community support", "Loneliness for me is usually the loss of family".

"Loneliness can best be understood as a signal coming from within ourselves that something is missing in our lives."[4] This missing something can take many forms; relationships with self, other, God, as well as a lack

---

[1] Russell et al., "Evolution."
[2] Jenny de Jong-Gierveld, "Developing and Testing a Model of Loneliness, <u>Journal of Personality and Social Psychology</u> 53 (1987): 119-128.
[3] Andersen.
[4] Bosaint, 324.

of meaning and purpose in one's life. As with broken relationships with people, a broken relationship with God is a very painful experience, most especially with those persons who dedicate their lives to a life in service of God.[5] This loneliness, a spiritual loneliness, is profound. It speaks to a deficiency in one's sense of spiritual well-being in two areas, in a sense of relatedness to God, and in one's sense of destiny and meaning in life.[6] Whatever is lacking, relationships to self, other, God, etc., all impact upon the person and result in some type of estrangement.   Emotional estrangement from significant others leads to an estrangement from self. Social estrangement leads to an estrangement from community. Each of these can lead to a sense of meaninglessness in life and ultimately lead to spiritual loneliness.

This present study shows, as in studies by Paloutzian et al., that there is a strong positive correlation between spiritual well-being with both existential well-being and religious well-being.[7] This adds support to the validity and reliability of the Spiritual Well-Being Scale to measure overall spiritual well-being along with religious well-being and existential well-being. The spiritual well-being scores for this population skew negatively having relatively high scores. These scores may be underestimated due to the ceiling affects for the Spiritual Well-Being Scale.[8] Ellison strongly supports the notion that one's intrinsic religious orientation is highly correlated with one's spiritual well-being. This is mostly due to one's sense of religious well-being.   Those who have internalized to a greater degree an intimate relationship to God have a higher sense of spiritual well-being.[9] One could reasonably assume that those persons who take an active role as a member of a religious congregation dedicated to God through service to the Church would likely have internalized their relationship with God. Paloutzian and Ellison tell us also that those whose religious commitment is very personal and intimate will likely have a good sense of overall well-being with a sense of purpose and meaning in their lives.[10] Persons who make a personal and intimate commitment to God, such as the women in this study, tend to have a greater sense of purpose and well-being present in their lives.   Having this greater sense of spiritual well-being impacts on the

---

[5] Kenel.
[6] Rokach, "Theoretical Approach."
[7] Paloutzian et al.
[8] Ledbetter et al.
[9] Ellison.
[10] Paloutzian et al.

level of loneliness. Those persons who have a personal commitment to God have shown lower levels of loneliness than did non-religious persons.[11] This phenomena is demonstrated in the data from this study where the levels of loneliness were positively skewed tending toward lower scores on the loneliness scale, and thus less loneliness. However, as has been cited, loneliness is a phenomenon that is an aspect of everyone's life at some time or other, and is so frightening to people that denial is often operative.[12]   While it is not clear whether or not the sisters had lower loneliness scores due to avoidance or denial, it seems that avoidance or denial was operative with persons who actually responded to the open ended question and those who did not complete the questionnaire but responded by letter. Examples of such responses are: "I'm not the lonely type," "I have no problem with loneliness, spiritual well-being, and community support," ". . . so many irons in the fire, that I have never found myself lonely except for the first two weeks after I left home for the convent," "I can't say I ever felt lonely. Coming from a large family, I was never alone," "I never felt lonely," "I have never felt lonely in religious life for I have always felt God with me, in me".

As shown in previous studies,[13] this study confirms that loneliness is negatively correlated to spiritual well-being. Given that spiritual well-being looks at the need for transcendence, that is the sense of well being that comes as a result of committing oneself in a manner that involves ultimate meaning in life on both a vertical scale, God related, and a horizontal scale, life satisfaction and purpose in life,[14] one may begin to delineate what dimensions are impacted upon when viewing the deficiencies in relationships that lead to loneliness. One can raise the question, is there a spiritual component to the experience of loneliness?

Dufton et al. conducted a study to see whether or not a relationship existed between religiosity and loneliness, and whether or not the person's faith enabled the person to cope with loneliness.[15] Three groups were studied, a non-religious group, a conservative religious group, and a non-conservative religious group. While these groups did not differ in their measures of loneliness, religious groups have found their ability to cope

---

[11] Ibid.
[12] Fromm-Reichmann; Moustakas; Sullivan; Mendelson.
[13] Ellison; Dufton et al.
[14] Ellison.
[15] Dufton et al.

with loneliness by using religious practices to buffer their experience. While the instruments in this study did not address religious practices, the comments of the sisters demonstrate that at least some of the respondents in this study found that their use of religious practices helped them to cope with loneliness, i.e., "Prayer group at this time (89-91) was a great aid", "I have made 10 years of directed retreats, a 30 day retreat, and I have X as a spiritual director", "I believe that loneliness is a part of our personal paschal mystery . . ." "I have great trust and confidence in the Lord, His Blessed Mother, and St. Joseph." Being or not being in relationship to self, other, God is most important in one's experience of loneliness and spiritual well-being.

Loneliness, Spiritual Well-Being and Social Networks

While this study supports findings about loneliness and spiritual well-being, only in part does it support the literature that shows the correlation between loneliness and social support. Two aspects of their networks that showed a statistically significant relationship were the total number of persons in their networks to whom they could turn to in an emergency and the number of significant negative relationships were in their network. The former has a negative correlation with loneliness and the latter a positive correlation with loneliness. It has been suggested by Stokes that the size of one's network should be related to and be a predictor of loneliness.[16] The larger the network of persons the less likely one should be lonely. While not the total number of persons in each sister's network, communal or personal, demonstrated this, the total number of those to whom they can turn to in an emergency does demonstrate such relationship. The more persons someone has to turn in a crisis, the less lonely they are likely to be.

Mellor et al. states that for the elderly two things appear to be predictors of loneliness, physical impairments and lack of confidants.[17] Given that 80% of the participants of this study were over the age of 50 it is important to address the issues of the loss of significant others and failing health and how this affects loneliness. While there was not a statistically significant correlation between the number of confidants and loneliness in

[16] Stokes.
[17] Mellor et al.

this study, there was a significant negative correlation between age and how much one socializes with friends and co-workers. This is understandable given the fact that as one ages, one's social network lessens and likely contributes to the experiences of loneliness. This was addressed by responses to the open ended question. Loss of their confidants, whether friend or family, brought about feelings of loneliness, as represented in the following comments: "Unfortunately my friends have preceded me to God and these were also my confidants", "My family lives in Europe. I have relied on friends both in and out of the community. The closest ones are dead", "Many of my friends have died which diminishes the number. I have other friends but we do not have contact at least once every two weeks". This loss of family and friends was reiterated over and over again. Many of these sisters, as noted in Chapter 4, suffered from impaired health, and thus have even more difficulty connecting to others, which leads to a feeling of isolation.

No other variable in either network showed any statistically significant relationship to loneliness either positive or negative, i.e., the number of confidants and the number of persons with whom one has a positive relationship, and the density of one's relationships. Why is this so? Williams et al. state that there is no difference between lonely or non-lonely people either in the number of best friends listed or the number of relationships that are reciprocal within the relationship.[18] This rationale may explain why the number of confidants and those with whom we have positive relations showed no significance in relationship to loneliness.

It is interesting to note that the number of persons one can turn to in an emergency has an impact on a person's level of loneliness, while the number of confidants one has does not. Relationships wherein one can turn to the other in an emergency may or may not be reciprocal in nature, but can be relied upon in a crisis. Having this type of networking would enable one to remain connected with another at difficult times, thereby, lessening the potential sense of isolation one might feel when facing a crisis alone. Confidants imply reciprocity and likely a continuous relationship over time. One might speculate that this type of relationship would by its very nature alleviate loneliness in self and other. In attempting to understand the results in relationship to confidants and how they may be different from those turned to in an emergency, there may be a number of mitigating factors. First, there were many who stated that the parameters of relating

[18] Williams et al.

with the person at least once every two weeks hampered their being able to list very significant persons/confidants in their lives that did not meet this restriction.   Thus this data may not reflect those with whom they have significant relationships, and may have resulted in listing some persons that they may not have otherwise listed, and may not have the high level of reciprocity that is related to less loneliness.[19]   There were many participants expressing this difficulty represented in the following comment of one participant:

> "I do not find these pages meaningful for me. The spectrum of ministry has brought me in contact with more lay persons who have been significant in my life but the every two weeks does not apply. There is one religious who has been a life long confidant whom I rarely see but is 'always there' if needed..."

Secondly, when studying support in its relationship to loneliness, the source of support or lack of it may come from factors other than those listed in the network listings. Mentioned often, for instance, was not having a place to list family members; and for many this was a main source of support.

Using the Spiritual Well-Being Scale and the network lists resulted in showing no statistically significant relationship between communal support and spiritual well-being. This does not support the literature that states that there is a strong relationship between the two. Israel et al., state that "the size, density, reciprocity, and geographic dispersion contribute significantly to psychological well-being."[20]   Given that authors such as Moberg and Hately tell us that spiritual well-being pertains to the wellness of the whole person, one's values, and meaning making for the person, [21] one can and should place psychological and spiritual well-being together. Therefore a correlation between spiritual well-being and communal support should be apparent. Why is that not shown using the instruments for this study?

There are a number of reasons to consider when answering this question. First, the difficulty experienced in completing the social network

---

[19] Karen Rook, "Reciprocity of Social Exchange and Social Satisfaction Among Older Women," Personality and Social Psychology 52 (1987): 145-154.
[20] Israel et al., 461.
[21] Moberg; Hateley; Craig Ellison and Joel Smith, "Toward and Integrative Measure of Health and Well-Being," Journal of Psychology and Theology 19 (1991): 35-48..

list must be addressed. Nine percent of the population did not complete the matrices measuring density because they found it to be too difficult and complex. Many others completing the matrices also noted that they were not sure whether they did it correctly. How much this difficulty played a part in those who actually completed the networks is hard to determine. However, it could also be assumed that those who completed the network lists without comment had no difficulty in doing so. They certainly, for the most part, represent a large percentage of the sample size.

Secondly, the directions on the network listing that specified using only those persons with whom they communicate at least once every two weeks, as well as not directly naming family as possible answers in the personal network list, was a deterrent for many, and as a result it may not reflect their true communal and personal networks, and therefore, would not show a statistically significant relationship to their sense of spiritual well-being.

Thirdly, the social network lists may not measure truly what is significant in relationship to communal support and spiritual well-being. The fact that there is a significant correlation between these two phenomena in the data gathered about their experience of loneliness, spiritual well-being, and communal support from 1960 to the present shows that indeed there is a relationship. Therefore there is reason to wonder more fully about why the networks themselves did not show any significance.

This study did not address individual differences which in some way may help us understand why the results were negligible. "Social support might have widely different personal meaning for people depending on their personalities, cognitive styles, and social histories."[22] Stokes tells us that experiences such as depression or low self esteem have a tremendous impact.[23] The need to address individual differences is supported by Newcomb as well. He tells us that "social support is both an aspect of the lifelong trajectory of social development, but is also shared and expressed in immediate transactions between individual characteristics and the responsiveness of the other in the immediate situation."[24] While this study

---

[22] Irwin Sarason et al., "Social Support: The Search for Theory," Journal of Social and Clinical Psychology 9 (1990): 134.

[23] Ibid.

[24] Michael Newcomb, "Social Support and Personal Characteristics: A Development and Interactional Perspective," Journal of Social and Clinical Psychology 9 (1990): 56.

did not address individual differences, the written responses to the open ended question as to whether or not there is more they thought should be addressed about loneliness, indicates that individual differences is an important factor and is represented in the following comments. "I took a sabbatical . . .I became very depressed . . .my self image was very low . . .I blamed myself as a failure". "I have had a lot of community support during my life time. I found that my loneliness sprang from inside me . . . and began a long inner journey . . ." "The first time I ever experienced hate . . . it was the first time to feel unrest and not be able to trust. God has always been my best friend and I experienced consolation from Him".

Along with individual differences one also notes that the situations in which the sister finds herself also impact on her loneliness, spiritual well-being and communal support, i.e., "The nature of work was very isolated and I did not at all enjoy either assignment . . .", "The 2 (a rating of low) in support was really lack of faculty support by one sister in each case who brought it home to the community", "There are periods in here in which there were eras of lack of corporate communal support in which some of us formed alternative communal gatherings. In addition there have sometimes been ministerial stress or well-being that has offset the communal experience . . .", "Congregational involvement aids my spiritual well-being and prevents loneliness", "My ministry satisfaction and/or level of stress in ministry affected spiritual well-being and loneliness".

Another reason to be considered as to why communal support and spiritual well-being did not show any significant relationship is the cultural dimension. Kenel speaks of the relationship of cultural changes, transitions in life and the social dimension of loneliness. These times sometimes "complicate and frustrate social and interpersonal communication."[25] While the instruments used in this study do not measure such a dimension, the responses of some of the sisters addressed it as important to be noted, i.e., ". . . after 20 years in the third world the reentry was painful and the greatest trial was that of loneliness. Not that the sisters were not kind,...they did not understand the trauma that accompanies 're-entry' (sic)"!

It is vitally important to take all factors into account to give a more complete picture in understanding loneliness. The literature finds that one's health, particularly one's well-being, spiritually and psychologically, as well

[25] Kenel, 716.

as one's level of loneliness, has been related to the availability of ties such as number of ties in a network, the frequency with which they come in contact with another, the type of relationship, density of network, and level of reciprocity.[26] Given these factors, the question surfaces, do these three phenomena have any factors that they share in common? While one must be cautious in interpreting the strength of the factors found in this study, they merit consideration.

Factoral Analysis

When the variables of loneliness, spiritual well-being, existential well-being were used in a factor analysis, three factors emerged. Factor one was the absence or perceived absence of connectedness to others; factor two was the absence or perceived absence of meaning and purpose in life, and factor three was the absence or perceived absence of a sense of cohesion and belonging. See table 4.1 for the variables that loaded onto each factor. One can see that variables loaded onto one and only one factor with the following exceptions: density loaded onto factors 1 and 3 in the personal network and on all three factors in the personal network; significant negative relationships loaded onto factors 2 and 3 in each network.

Variables in both networks, communal and personal, involving the number of confidants, persons they can turn to in an emergency, those persons who have a positive influence in their life and density load very strongly onto factor one, the lack of or absence of connectedness to others. The fewer the number of these types of relationships the less connected one feels; and the denser one's social network the less connected one feels to others. Reis tells us that interaction intimacy is the best predictor of social support. "Feeling connected with a caregiver who is reliable, sensitive, and responsive"[27] is needed for a sense of social support. Without interconnection with significant other/s, experiences of loneliness would increase and the experience of spiritual well-being decrease.[28] If strongly connected, why then did loneliness and spiritual

---

[26]Alacay; Stokes; B. Wellman, "Structural Analysis: From Method and Metaphor to Theory and Substance," in Social Structures and Social Support ed. Barry Wellman and S.D. Berkowitz (Cambridge: Cambridge University Press), 19-61.

[27]Harry Reis, "The Role of Intimacy in Interpersonal Relations," Journal of Social and Clinical Psychology 9 (1990): 17.

[28]Reis.

Table 4.1--Factor Loadings of Variables.

FACTOR ONE NON-CONNECTEDNESS	FACTOR TWO LACK OF MEANING	FACTOR THREE NONBELONGING
LACK OF HELPER IN AN	INCREASE IN	NEGATIVE
LACK OF A POSITIVE RELATIONSHIP	LACK OF SPIRITUAL WELL -BEING	INCREASE IN DENSITY
LACK OF A CONFIDANT	NEGATIVE RELATIONSHIPS	
INCREASE IN DENSITY	DECREASE IN DENSITY	

well-being not load onto factor one with the variables related to communal support?   This fact is not unfounded in the literature. Sarason et al. tell us that "the view of social support as interpersonal connectedness emphasizes the structure of the individual's social network and often leads to an analysis that focuses attention on relating quantitative descriptions of the social environment to . . . measures related to psychological adjustment and health status",[29] i.e., loneliness scales and spritiual well-being scales. "Available evidence suggests that social connectedness per se is often not a powerful factor in health and personal adjustment".[30]   If one moves beyond the structural factors of communal support, one may find more common ground when related to such experiences as spiritual well-being and loneliness. Carson et al. speak of characteristics of spiritual well-being in such a manner.   One of these characteristics is "a common bond between individuals which allows the sharing of warmth, love and compassion, a commitment to God, the performance of unselfish acts, and the adherence to a set of ethical principles . . ." [31]

As has been said many times already, loneliness and spiritual well-being are negatively correlated with one another. This correlation is shown again in the factor analysis, where one sees that loneliness loads strongly

[29]Sarason et al., 135.
[30]Ibid., 135.
[31]Carson et al., 161.

and consistently with spiritual well-being, existential well-being, and religious well-being. Spiritual well-being, existential well-being, and religious well-being address relatedness with self, other, and God in a manner that gives meaning and purpose in life. Thus the loneliness addressed here reflects a spiritual well-being lacking in meaning and purpose due to the absence or perceived absence of the Ultimate Other the source of all meaning in life. One can be lonely when "the person experiences a feeling of being out of touch with an ultimate source of life and meaning."[32] This is a source that Frankl tells us, as reported by Soderstrom et al., is a "basis for the discovery of meaning and purpose in life."[33]   Soderstrom et al.in their study of mature religious commitment and their search for meaning in life, found that religious commitment is indicative of greater meaning in life, where a lack of this commitment shows less meaning in life.[34] Given that the population studied here are women who have made a religious commitment that is vital to their lives, it is understandable that meaning and purpose and one's experience of loneliness would be closely aligned with one another.

The third factor, the lack or absence of a sense of belonging and cohesion, is strongly related to density and the number of persons in a given network who have a negative relationship to the individual. The greater the density within a sister's network the less likely she is to feel that she belongs, and the more likely she is to have a significant negative relationship. Density in this factor analyis results in the opposite of what one would expect since the literature states that the more dense one's network the less lonely one would feel. This again may be the result of the difficulty many had in filling out the netwok questionnaires, making it difficult to know whether or not these results have any substantive meaning. One could, however, wonder if a denser relationship network can result in feeling a sense of isolation or loneliness because one is sharing friends with another when one is not involved in all aspects of the relationships of persons in her network.

Another question to be considered is why the variables addressing particular types of relationships load onto factor one, the lack or absence of connectedness to others, and not onto factor three, a feeling of not

---

[32]Bonsaint, 323.
[33]Doug Soderstrom and E. Wayne Wright, "Religious Orientation and Meaning in Life," Journal of Clinical Psychology 33 (1977): 65.
[34]Ibid.

belonging to a significant group? Consider two possibilities. Firstly, it is possible that one can feel connected to individuals and still not feel a part of the group as a whole, and secondly just as loneliness had dimensions beyond feeling connected, so too does belonging go beyond connectedness to others. It addresses a need for a common core experience, working for a common vision as a group. This study did not address this facet of the community and personal network. Due to its structural and quantitative nature, limitations for drawing conclusions in this regard are significant.

When looking at religious well-being apart from spiritual well-being and existential well-being, differences in understanding the factors occur. Again the variables clearly align themselves onto one factor the few exceptions noted in chapter 4, statistical findings. See table 4.2. The first factor remains the same in content and interpretation, but differences arise in factors two and three. Again loneliness aligns itself with religious well-being, just as it did with spiritual well-being and existential well-being. In this instance loneliness and religious well-being fall onto factor three, an absence or lack of relatedness to God. In this instance we are looking at another aspect of loneliness, i.e., spiritual loneliness. This can be interpreted as "being out of touch with an ultimate source of life and meaning."[35] It is on this level that loneliness takes on a specifically religious form, a desire to transcend this type of loneliness is the desire to feel the presence of God and not God's absence.[36] Factor 2 in this instance is a sense of isolation of self and isolation from the positive significant other. This isolation is intensified with the presence of negative significant relationships. Isolation of self from the other leads to both and emotional and social estrangement.[37] There is experienced in this estrangement a lack of intimacy with individuals and a lack of feeling bonded to a group. In women religious this experience often leads to a sense of marginality with their congregations.

The unidimensionality of loneliness must be questioned based upon the results of this factor analysis. There in fact appear to be several dimensions present. While the loneliness measured by UCLA Loneliness Scale (Version Three) is thought to be unidimensional, one can also begin

[35]Bonsaint, 323.
[36]Ibid.
[37]Andersen.

Table 4.2.--Factor Loadings of Variables.

FACTOR ONE ON-CONNECTEDNESS	FACTOR TWO ISOLATION OF SELF/OTHER	FACTOR THREE ABSENCE OF GOD
ACK OF HELPER IN AN MERGENCY	NEGATIVE RELATIONSHIPS	LONELINESS
ACK OF A POSITIVE ELATIONSHIP	SMALLER DENSITY	LACK OF RELIGIOUS WELL - BEING
ACK OF A CONFIDANT		NEGATIVE RELATIONSHIPS
		DECREASED DENSITY
CREASED DENSITY		

to speculate that it addresses a number of factors given that it aligns itself quite strongly with spiritual well-being, existential well-being, and religious well-being. There appear to be four factors to consider: the absence or perceived absence of the Ultimate Other; the absence or perceived absence of meaning and purpose in life; the absence or percieved absence of connectedness to significant others resulting in an isolation of self; and an absence or perceived absence of a sense of belonging resulting in an isolation from others. See figure 4.1. These findings may give some support to Austin's notion that the UCLA Loneliness Scale measures several facets of loneliness.[38] He found three factors in relationship to loneliness; intimate others, social others, and a feelings of a lack of belonging and affiliation. The factors found to be strongly allied with loneliness in this study are the absence or perceived absence of the Ultimate Other, and the absence or perceived absence of meaning and purpose in life. Ellison states that beyond the necessity for having, relating, and being, a fourth need for transcendence needs to be addressed.[39] "This refers to the sense of well-being that we experience when we find purposes to commit ourselves to that which involve ultimate meaning in life."[40] Whether one feels isolated from, alienated from, or abandoned by the Ultimate Other, the loneliness experienced in particular instances is extremely painful leading to

---

[38]Bruce Austin, "Factorial Structure of the UCLA Loneliness Scale,"PsychologicalReports 53 (1983): 883-889.
    [39]Ellison.
    [40]Ibid., 330.

Figure 4.1.-- Dimensions of Loneliness

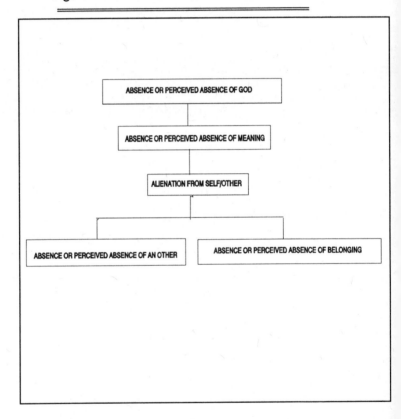

an isolated self from which one has great difficulty escaping.[41]

> The sense of a broken relationship with God is a painful experience for anyone, but perhaps more especially for religious who have dedicated their entire lives and being to fostering that relationship and making it of central importance...The sense of God's absence, then, creates a gap that cannot be filled simply by human companionship. It may be that the failure to properly identify this form of loneliness leads to disillusionment with community. [42]

Frankl strongly asserts that the transcendental need for meaning and commitment in life is essential to health and well-being.[43] Religious commitment, he tells us, is indicative of greater meaning in life. It is not surprising, therefore, that the population for this study, women who have strong religious commitments, find that the presence of the Ultimate Other is vital to bring meaning and purpose in life and without this loneliness likely occurs.

Religious Life from 1960 - 1991

Continuing to look at women who make a religious commitment to serve God within a particular religious congregation, and viewing religious life from 1960 to the present, adds another dimension to this study. This dimension uses the data that views religious life during this time period with regard to loneliness, spiritual well-being, and communal support in relationship to leadership style, manner of deciding one's residence, as well as time frames in defined segments. In order to understand the overall results more clearly, this data has been divided into time periods that represent many of the changes that have occurred since the second Vatican Council. 1960-66 represents a period noted by many to be quite turbulent. At this time there were in "the United States 181,000 sisters and nuns in over 500 different religious congregations and orders."[44] The Vatican council decreed that religious congregations begin a renewal of their lives by returning to their roots and understanding the mission and

---

[41]Sobosan.

[42]Mary Elizabeth Kenel, "Community: Problems of Loneliness and Ambivalence," Review for Religious 42 (1983):713-721.

[43]Frankl.

[44]Marie Augusta Neal, From Nuns to Sisters an Expanding Vocation (Mystic: Twenty-Third Publications, 1990), 31.

charism of their congregations as perceived by their founders and foundresses. As a result, "there followed the special General Chapters to deliberate the agenda of renewal, moving toward constitutional updating." [45] This was a time marked by changes in such things as style of dress, types of ministry sisters were involved in, and developing new ways of living together such as moving out of convents into apartments. Many of these changes represented giving up what many felt to be sacred and unchangeable.

The second period of years is 1967-76. Membership in congregations reached its peak in 1966, and then there was a sharp decline.[46] During this time religious congregations began to experience the exodus of large numbers of sisters. For some, progress was not fast enough; for some it was too fast; and some realized that religious life was no longer their life choice. The freedom to leave without being stigmatized and/or spirited away in secret occurred as well. There were many hypotheses as to the reasons for the decline. Neal cites several such as, "the opening of the church to lay women and men, eager to participate after the Second Vatican Council had recognized their baptismal calling to church work, certainly partially explains the trends."[47] Women could begin taking an active role in the Church outside of religious congregations.

In the period from 1977 to 1986, there was a growing awareness of oppression in our own country with civil rights violations and the oppression in the third world countries and the call to serve the poor which brought about a focus on a global scale with less focus on the internal life of the congregation. Increased numbers of sisters took active roles in fighting oppression by taking part in protests through civil disobedience. This was a very difficult time in the history of religious life. What it meant to serve the poor and fight oppression was a very important but difficult question to answer.

The latter years, from 1987 to the present, finds religious congregations grappling with what it means to be women religious in today's society. Greater participation in decision making exists. Religious life today is suffering with dwindling numbers and is faced with a

[45]Ibid., 57.
[46]Ibid.
[47]Ibid. 33.

tremendous increase in aging members. While congregations continue to grow in the understanding that one's focus or mission in the church must be global and more other centered, worries and fears about how they will function, what form religious life will take, and whether or not the individual congregations will survive in the future are vital issues that all face.

Consistent with other findings in this study, we find again that loneliness is negatively correlated with spiritual well-being and communal support, and spiritual well-being and communal support are positively correlated with one another. When the chi-square levels of significance were calculated there were no statistically significant relationships between loneliness and leadership style, method of choosing residence, or the year in which a particular residence began. While one must be cautious in analysis, this may add continued support to the earlier findings that loneliness for this population is more directly related to an absence of the Ultimate Other and a lack of meaning in one's life than to method of choice and leadership style.

Cautiousness in the following discussion is also necessary for a number of other reasons. There has been no study of this nature where an attempt has been made to see the impact of the many changes in religious life from 1960 to the present in relationship to loneliness, spiritual well-being, and communal support. Such a study involves recall of experiences over a 31 year span. The degree of accuracy in terms of the actual experience is difficult to measure. For instance, negative experiences may have lessened in their intensity as they receded into past memory. Because it is difficult to experience loneliness and often the desire to deny is present, the original experience may no longer be thought of in a negative light. Positive experiences may also be muted over time, and could possibly be viewed as more negative later on due to additional negative life experiences. Also to be considered is the fact that when there are a large number of entries of data using chi-square statistical tests, the data may tend to show a higher degree of significance than actually exists. Results are limited in their interpretation, but are not to be ignored.

The average number of years for each place of residence was 5.5, and the average number of sisters within each residence was 23. While the data shows no statistically significant relationship between loneliness, spiritual well-being and communal support and the number of years one stays in a residence, and the average number of sisters with whom one lives, the comments raised by sisters in this regard merit consideration. In terms of the number of residents within a given house the responses are mixed. Some found that small houses were more life producing than large houses and vice versa, i.e., "In a large house situation a person can become very lonely - they can be lost in the struggle", "I have found that living in a small setting is not my way of living. I prefer a larger group and am in the process of moving to a new location for next year", "Now that I no longer live in an institutional setting, loneliness has abated considerably. I feel positive, happy, hopeful most of the time", "I live and work in a small group of 7, one of 6 groups in the house of approximately 60 sisters. I do little socializing apart from my small group...I enjoy being with the sisters, small and large, but am not really close to many", "When I left X . . . after many years and went to a small living community, it was hard as all my friends in religion were in X . . . I had to start all over again".

It was not the number of years that a person remained in a residence that was problematic, it was rather the transition from one residence to another that was most difficult. Transitions and the feelings around the many moves sisters had to make over the years was never openly addressed. One was expected to simply adapt. It was God's will. The realization that transitions surfaced feelings of loneliness and loss was not acknowledged and any mention of it was taboo.[48] A person was readily changed from one place to the other for the common good of the whole. It was not uncommon for sisters to change residences year to year and sometimes the length of time was even less. This frequent movement was also difficult for those sisters who remained in a given house because the make-up of the house would change as new sisters joined them. In the following quotations one can see the struggle in transitioning from one place to another or remaining in one place while new members joined the living group: "This is extremely difficult for me. If a living situation was supportive one year the support could transition out the next". "When assigned from one convent to another it was always because the convent closed so I had to adjust to a completely new environment as well as community. This last place has been the most lonely for me. I feel very little support". "I feel loneliness may be brought on an individual's transition from one community/ministry to another", "There are periods in here in which there were eras of a lack of corporate communal support in which some of us formed alternative communal gatherings".

---

[48]Marie Conn, "The Loneliness of Transition", Review for Religious 45 (1986): 293-295.

The chi-square results showed a statistically significant frequency of those who rate support and spiritual well-being at a five, very high for the time period 1987-1991. While this is a difficult time in religious life, religious groups have a more active stance which results in a sense of empowerment about the present and the future. As Neal states, there is a new dynamic in religious life. Her scientific research and analysis showed "that sisters perceive the following as fundamental to their contemporary mission: 1) learning responsible participation based on interdependency rather than dependency; 2) a recognition of new authority, shaped and grounded in trained and apostolically committed competency; 3) a shared use of human skills; and 4) other insights of resourceful collegial governance in behalf of the mission of the church.[49]

Data collected by a survey from Catholic religious congregations of women in the United States in 1966 and 1982 delineated changes in leadership style from 1966 and 1982.[50] In 1966 the majority of congregations' local superiors, 81.1%, were appointed by the major superior without consultation. In 1982 this was only true for .9% of congregations. The question as to whether or not there was a local superior was not a question that would even be considered in 1966. By 1982 there were 25.4% of local houses with no local superior. In this present study for the years from 1986-1991, 72.5 percent of the sisters live/d in houses that were collegial in leadership style, and only 11% lived in houses where there were local superiors. There was a significant increase in the frequencies of sisters rating their level of support and spiritual well-being as very high and high respectively for those sisters living in houses where the governmental process was collegial in nature. One might speculate that while changes have been very difficult, religious women have grown a great deal in the process leading to a more general overall feeling of well-being and support. It was a struggle, as Neal points out, "to leave the old restraints behind us drawing us into relationships where we needed to learn or re-learn how to relate and communicate with others leading us to the interaction that creates communal bonds of understanding and communication among people who work and live together."[51]

Along with more participative government comes the persons

---

[49]Neal, 95.

[50]Marie Augusta Neal, Catholic Sisters in Transition from the 1960s to the 1980s, (Wilmington:Michael Glazier, Inc.,1984), vol.2, Consecrated Life Studies.

[51]Neal, From Nuns to Sisters, 79.

proactive choice as to where one will live. Approximately eighty six percent of the persons in this study at the present time have chosen their place of residence, a move Keyes tells us may prove very helpful.[52] Stress in the living situation can cause, according to Keyes, a withdrawal from the community setting. Choice can at least to some degree eliminate the stress caused by a negative living experience within the local community. It can offer us a sense of well-being and belonging making the life experience of the sister more fulfilling.[53] This may help one to understand why there appears to be a statistically significant frequency of those who experience high and very high ratings of spiritual well-being and communal support in those who have chosen their place of residence.

There are of course many other facets of religious life that would merit it study. This study is a beginning for viewing religious life in the past three decades in relationship to loneliness, spiritual well-being, and social support. It gives a base for reflection and dialogue about their importance and their integral weaving with our lives. It helps us to see that these are not discrete phenomena, but rather weave a tapestry that intertwines them.

[52]Ralph Keyes, We,the Lonely People (New York: Harper and Row, 1973), 720.
[53]Nouwen, 32.

CHAPTER FIVE

TYING THE THREADS TOGETHER

What are the implications for religious congregations as a result of this study? There are a number of them. Loneliness, spiritual well-being, and communal support are intricately connected to one another. They impact upon one's relationship to God; one's sense of meaning and purpose in life; one's feeling connected to significant others; and one's ability to feel a part of the community. It is important to address each of them in relationship to one another.

Loss and transitions are significant issues within congregations and will impinge upon one's overall sense of well-being. The concerns are twofold. First, with the many transitions in religious life as a result of Vatican II, and the uncertainty of how religious life will look in the future, we are impelled to be attuned to the profound ways in which loss through change and transition can impact upon our lives. While spiritual well-being appears to enable the individual sister to cope with loneliness, drawing on an intimate relationship with God, the failure to address such important issues can lead to loneliness and isolation and a questioning of one's meaning and purpose in life.

Congregations have increasing numbers of elderly. As one ages one is faced more losses; the death of loved ones, loss of community members, family members, and friends. This will undoubtedly impact upon one's sense of well-being and feelings of support within the congregation. There is a tendency to avoid dealing with the pain of loss openly. The process of working through these issues as individuals and congregations openly allows feelings of support and overall well-being to work positively and hopefully in times of difficulty and will bring healing to those who are in pain from recent loss as well as those who have carried pain from many losses in the past.

There are indications that those sisters who take an active part in decision making and reside in houses where the leadership style is collegial in nature have a greater sense of spiritual well-being and communal support. This may serve as a guideline for promoting healthier individuals and ultimately healthier congregations.

<u>Recommendations for Further Research</u>

There are a number of areas to consider for further research.

Another study needs to be done with male clergy and religious congregations of men. This would aid in exploring gender differences in the experiences of loneliness, spiritual well-being and social/communal support.

A qualitative research approach to studying loneliness, spiritual well-being, and communal support may aid in developing a more in depth understanding of these phenomena.

Given that personality traits have been shown to impact upon levels of loneliness, spiritual well-being, and ultimately communal support, the use of personality inventories should also be included in a study of these phenomena.

This study dealt with a limited aspect of religious life, namely communal support. Aspects such as prayer life and the vows of poverty, chastity, and obedience have not been addressed. A study using a broader scope of religious life would add valuable knowledge to the understanding of loneliness, spiritual well-being, and communal support.

Exploring more fully a multi-dimensional study of loneliness with the absence or perceived absence of God as an important facet would be very valuable.

A more in depth study of how good health or the lack of it impacts on one's level of loneliness, spiritual well-being, and community support would add to the depth of knowledge about these phenomena.

As religious congregations move into the future with many uncertainties, a longitudinal study of loneliness, spiritual well-being, and communal support would be of value.

A multi-cultural study should be done to determine whether or not different cultures experience these phenomena differently.

Further research can include all areas in the United States to determine if there are any significant differences in the experiences of loneliness, spiritual well-being, and communal support in religious congregations of men and women as well as clergy outside of religious congregations.

It is the hope of this author that this study has offered a significant piece of research to the field pastoral psychology. It offers the opportunity t view the integral relationship between loneliness, spiritual well-being, and communal support as experienced by women in religious congregations. It is an opportunity to reflect on these phenomena in a way that opens dialogue with religious congregations about topics that tend to be avoided . It will hopefully engender thinking about what helps one to live a life with a sense of overall well-being as individual members and as total congregations.

BIBLIOGRAPHY

Alcalay, Rina. "Health and Social Support Networks: A Case for Improving Interpersonal Communication." Social Networks 5 (1983): 71-88.

Andersen, Lars. "A Model of Estrangement: Including a Theoretical Understanding of Loneliness." Psychological Reports 58 (1986): 683-695.

Aschenbrenner, George. "A Celibate's Relationship with God." Human Development 5 (1984): 38-43.

_____. "Celibacy in Community and Ministry." Human Development 6 (1985): 27-33.

Austin, Bruce. "Factorial Structure of the UCLA Loneliness Scale." Psychological Reports 53 (1983): 883-889.

Barden, Arden. "Toward New Directions for Ministry in Aging: An Overview of Issues and Concepts." Journal of Religion and Aging 1-2 (1986): 137-149.

Bonsaint, Romeo. "Loneliness: The Experience of Social Alienation. Studies in Formative Spirituality 5 (1984): 323-333.

Bowlby, John. "Affectional bonds." In Loneliness: The Experience of Emotional and Social Isolation. ed. R.Weiss. 38-52. Cambridge: MIT Press.

Breiger, Ronald. "The Duality of Persons and Groups." In Social Structures: A Network Approach. eds. B. Wellman and S. Berkowitz. 83-98. Cambridge: Cambridge University Press.

Brownell, Arlene and Sally Ann Schumaker. "Social Support: An Introduction to a Complex Phenomenon." Journal of Social Issues 40 (1984): 1-9.

Bufford, Rodger, Paloutzian, Raymond, and Craig Ellison. "Norms for the Spiritual Well-Being Scale." 1990. Western Baptist Seminary and The Alliance Theological Seminary.

Cada, Lawrence. Shaping the Coming Age of Religious Life. New York: Seabury Press. 1979.

Carson, Verna, Soeken, Karen, and Patricia Grimm. "Hope and its Relationship to Spiritual Well-Being." Journal of Psychology and Theology 16 (1988): 159-167.

Cioffi, Karen. "Loneliness: A Painful Blessing." Spiritual Life 34 (1988): 144-45.

Coetzee, Jan. "The Manifestation of Religious Commitment with Regard to Divergent Reality Definitions." In Spiritual Well-Being: Sociological Perspectives, ed. David Moberg, 291-300. Washington. DC: University Press, 1979.

Conn, Marie. "The Loneliness of Transition." Review for Religious 45 (1986): 293-295.

Coyne, James and Niall Bolger. "Doing Without Social Support as an Explanatory Concept." Journal of Social and Clinical Psychology 9 (1990): 148-158.

de Jong-Gierveld, Jenny. "Developing and Testing a Model of Loneliness." Journal of Personality and Social Psychology 53 (1987): 119-128.

Derlega, Valerian and S. Margulis. "Why Loneliness Occurs: The Interrelationship of Social Psychological and Privacy Concepts." In Loneliness: A Sourcebook of Current Theory, Research, and Therapy, eds. Letitia Peplau and Daniel Perlman, 152-165. New York: John Wiley & Sons, 1982.

Dufton, Brian and Daniel Perlman. "Loneliness and Religiosity: In the World but Not of It." The Journal of Psychology and Theology 14 (1986): 135-145.

Ellison, Craig and Joel Smith. "Toward and Integrative Measure of Health and Well-Being." Journal of Psychology and Theology 19 (1991): 35-48.

Ellison, Craig. "Spiritual Well-Being: Conceptualization and Measurement." Journal of Psychology and Theology 11 (1983): 330-340.

_____. "Loneliness: A Social-Developmental Analysis." Journal of Psychology and Theology 6 (1978): 3-16.

Flannery, Austin. Decree on the Up to Date Renewal of Religious Life. Vatican Council II: The Conciliar Documents. Translated by A. Flannery. Northport: Costello Publishing Co., 1975.

Frankl, Victor. The Unconscious God. New York: Simon and Schuster, 1975.

Fromm-Reichmann, Frieda. "Loneliness." In The Anatomy of Loneliness, eds. Joseph Hartog and Yehuda Cohen,338-361. New York: International Universities Press, 1980.

Garret, W. "Reference Groups and Role Strains Related to Spiritual Well-Being." In Spiritual Well-Being: Sociological Perspectives, ed., David Moberg. 73-89. Washington, DC: University Press. 1979.

Gay, L. R. Educational Research: Competencies for Analysis and Application , 3rd ed., Columbus: Merrill Publishing Company, 1987.

George, Jeanne. "Loneliness in the Priesthood." Human Development 10 (1989): 12-15.

Hateley, B.. "Spiritual Well-Being Through Life Histories." Journal of Religious and Aging 1 (1985): 62-71.

Heller, Kenneth and William Mansbach. "The Multifaceted Nature of Social Support in a Community Sample of Elderly Women." Journal of Social Issues 40 (1984). 99-112.

Hinkle, Dennis, Wiersma, William, and Stephen Jurs. Applied Statistics for the Behavioral Sciences. 2nd ed. Boston: Houghton Mifflin Company. 1988..

Hirsch, Barton. "Psychological Dimensions of Social Networks: A Multimethod Analysis." American Journal of Community Psychology 7 (1979): 263-277.

_____. "Social Networks and the Coping Process: Creating Personal Communities." In Social Networks and Social Support. ed. Benjamin Gottleib. 149-170. Beverly Hills: Sage Publications. 1981.

Hsu, Lorie, Hailey, B. Jo, and Lillian Range. "Cultural and Emotional Components of Loneliness and Depression." The Journal of Psychology 121 (1986): 61-70.

Hungelmann, JoAnn, Eileen Kenkel-Rossi, Loretta Klassen, and Ruth Stollenwerk. "Spiritual Well-Being in Older Adults: Harmonious Interconnectedness." Journal of Religious and Health 24 (1990): 147-153.

Israel, Barbara and Toni Antonucci. "Social Network Characteristics and Psychological Well-Being: A Replication and Extension." Health Education Quarterly 14 (1987): 461-481.

Kelsey, Kelley. "The Gift of Loneliness." Spirituality Today 36. (1984): 100-108.

Kenel, Mary Elizabeth. "Community: Problems of Loneliness and Ambivalence." Review for Religious 42 (1983): 713-721.

Kerlinger, Fred. Foundations of Behavioral Research, 2d ed., New York: Holt, Rinehart, and Winston, Inc.. 1983.

_____ and Elazar Pedhezau. Multiple Regression in Behavioral Research. New York: Holt, Rinehart, and Winston, Inc. 1973.

Keyes, Ralph. We, the Lonely People. New York: Harper and Row. 1973.

Kim, Jae-on, and Charles Mueller. Introduction to Factor Analysis: What it is and How to do it. Beverly Hills: Sage Publications. 1978.

_____. Factor analysis: Statistical Methods and Practical issues. Beverly Hills: Sage Publications. 1978..

Ledbetter, Mark, Leslie Smith, Hunter Vosler, L. Wanda, and James Fischer. "An Evaluation of the Research and Clinical Usefulness of the Spiritual Well-Being Scale." Journal of Psychology and Theology 19 (1991): 49-55.

Lozano, John. "Trends in Religious Life Today." Review for Religious 42 (1983): 481-503.

Marcum, Regina. "Religious Women's Communities and Spiritual Well-Being." In Spiritual Well-Being: Sociological Perspectives, ed., David Moberg, 265-279. Washington, DC: University Press. 1979.

Markham, Donna. "Communal Life and Global Reality." Human Development 8 (1987): 14-19.

McNamara, Patrick and Arthur St. George. "Measures of Religiosity and the Quality of Life: A Critical Analysis." In Spiritual Well-Being: Sociological Perspectives, ed., David Moberg, 229-236. Washington, DC: University Press. 1979.

Mellor, Karen and Robert Edelman. "Mobility. SocialSupport, Loneliness and Well-Being Amongst Two Groups of Older Adults." Personality and Individual Differences 9 (1988): 1-5.

Mendelson, Myer. "Reflections on Loneliness." Contemporary Psychoanalysis 26 (1990): 330-354.

Mitchell, Roger and Edison Trickett. "Task Force Report: Social Networks as Mediators of Social Support: An Analysis of the Effects and Determinants of Social Networks." Community Mental Health Journal 16 (1980): 27-44.

Moberg, David. "The Developemnt of Social Indicators of Spiritual Well-Being for Quality of Life Research." In Spiritual Well-Being: Sociological Perspectives, ed., David Moberg, 1-13. Washington, D.C.: University Press. 1979.

Moffet, Patrick. "Marginality and Religious Life: Belonging to a Group Called to Risk." Review for Religious 43 (1984): 842-848.

Moustakas, Clark. Loneliness. New York: Prentice Hall Inc.. 1961.

Neal, Marie Augusta. "Catholic Sisters in Transition from the 1960's to 1980's". Vol 2. Consecrated Life Studies. Wilmington: Michael Glazier, Inc.. 1984.

_____. From Nuns to Sisters an Expanding Vocation. Mystic: Twenty-Third Publications. 1990.

Neale, Robert. Loneliness, Solitude, and Companionship. Philadelphia: Westminster Press. 1984.

Newcomb, Michael and Bentler, Peter. "Loneliness and Social Support: A Confirmatory Hierarchical Analysis. Personality and Social Psychology Bulletin 12 (1986): 520-535.

Newcomb Michael. "Social Support and Personal Characteristics: A Developmental and Interactional Perspective." Journal of Social and Clinical Psychology 9 (1990): 54-68.

Nouwen, Henry. Reaching Out: The Three Movements of the Spiritual Life. Garden City: Doubleday & Company, Inc.. 1978.

Omodio, Frances. (1986). Loneliness and Friendship in Religious Life. Sisters Today. 58. 160-163.

Paloutzian, Raymond and Craig Ellison. "Loneliness, Spiritual Well-Being and the Quality of Life." in Loneliness: A Sourcebook of Current Theory, Research and Therapy, ed., Letitia Peplau and Daniel Perlman. 234-237. New York: John Wiley & Sons, 1982.

Parkes, C. Murray. "Separation Anxiety: An Aspect of the Search of the Lost Object." in Loneliness: The Experience of Emotional and Social Isolation, ed., Robert Weiss. 53-68. Cambridge: MIT Press, 1973.

Peplau, Letitia, Miceli, Maria, and Bruce Morasch. "Loneliness and Self-Evaluation." in Loneliness: A Sourcebook of Current Theory, Research and Therapy, ed., Letitia Peplau and Daniel Perlman, 135-151. New York: John Wiley & Sons, 1982.

Peplau, Letitia and Daniel Perlman. "Perspectives on Loneliness," in Loneliness: A Sourcebook of Current Theory, Research and Therapy, ed., Letitia Peplau and Daniel Perlman, 2-12. New York: John Wiley & Sons, 1982.

Polcino, Anna. Loneliness: The Genesis of Solitude, Friendship, and Contemplation (Whitinsville: Affirmation Press. 1979).

Powell, F.C. Statistical Tables for the Social, Biological,and Physical Sciences (New York: Cambridge University Press, 1982).

Reis, Harry. "The Role of Intimacy in Interpersonal Relations."The Journal of Social and Clinical Psychology 9 (1990): 15-30.

Ripple, Paula. "Saying Yes to Life: Saying Yes to Relationships." Studies in Formative Spirituality 6 (1985): 387-397.

Rokach, Ami. "The Experience of Loneliness: A Tri-Level Model." The Journal of Psychology 122 (1988): 531-543.

_____. "Antecedents of Loneliness: A Factorial Analysis." Journal of Psychology 123 (1989): 369-384.

_____. "Theoretical Approaches to Loneliness: From a Univariate to a Multidimensional Experience." Review of Existential Psychology and Psychiatry 19 (1984-85): 225-247.

Rook, Karen. "Research on Social Support, Loneliness, and Social Isolation." Review of Personality and Social Psychology 5 (1984): 239-264.

_____. "Reciprocity of Social Exchange and Social Satisfaction Among Older Women." Personality and Social Psychology 52 (1987): 145-154.

Roscoe, John. Fundamental Research Statistics for the Behavioral Sciences. New York: Holt, Rinehart, and Winston, Inc.. 1969.

Rosen, Allison. "Fromm-Reichmann's Last Paper." Contemporary Psychoanalysis 26 (1990): 356-360.

Russell, Dan, Carolyn Cutrona, Jayne Rose, and Karen Yurko. "Social and Emotional Loneliness: An Examination of Weiss's Typology of Loneliness." Journal of Personality and Social Psychology 6 (1984): 1313-1321.

_____, Peplau, Letitia, and Carolyn Cutrona. "The Revised UCLA Loneliness Scale: Concurrent and Discriminant Validity Evidence." Journal of Personality and Social Psychology 39 (1980): 472-480.

86

_____, Altmaier, Elizabeth, and Dawn Van Velzen. "Job Related Stress, Social Support, and Burnout Among Classroom Teachers." The Journal of Applied Psychology 72 (1987): 269-274.

_____, Cutrona, C. Development and Evolution of the UCLA Loneliness Scale (Grants R01-AG03846 & PO1-AG07094 from the National Institute of Aging) Iowa: University of Iowa. Center for Health Services Research, College of Medicine. 1990.

Sabosan, Jeffrey. "Loneliness and Faith." Journal of Psychology and Theology 6 (1978): 104-108.

Sarason, Irwin, Sarason, Barbara, and Gregory Pierce."Social Support:The Search for Theory." The Journal of Social and Clinical Psychology 9 (1990): 133-147.

Savramis, Demosthenes. "Religion as Subjective Experience and Social Reality." in Spiritual Well-Being: Sociological Perspectives, ed., David Moberg. 119-131. Washington, DC: University Press, 1979.

Scalise, Joseph, Ginter, Earl, and Lawrence Gerstein. "A Multidimensional Loneliness Measure: The Loneliness Rating Scale (LRS)." Journal of Personality Assessment 48 (1984): 525-530.

Sheets, J. "The Consecrated Life." Communio 9 (1982):3-15.

Shinn, Marybeth, Lehmann, Stanley, and Nora Wong. "Social Interaction and Social Support." Journal of Social Issues 40 (1984): 55-76.

Shumaker, Sally and Arlene Brownell. "Toward a Theory of Social Support: Closing Conceptual Gaps." Journal of Social Issues 40 (1984): 11-36.

Siegel, Sidney. Nonparametric Statistics. New York: McGraw-Hill, Inc.. 1956.

Soderstrom. Doug, and E. Wayne Wright. "Religious Orientation and Meaning of Life." Journal of Clinical Psychology 33 (1977): 65-68.

Spatz, Chris and James Johnston. Basic Statistics: Tales of Distributions. 3rd ed.. (Monterey: Brooks/Cole Publishing Company, 1984).

Stokes, Joseph. "The Relation of Social Network and Individual Difference Variables to Loneliness." Journal of Personality and Social Psychology 48 (1985): 981-990.

Stokes, Joseph and Ira Levin. "Gender Differences in Predicting Loneliness from Social Network Characteristics." Journal of Personality and Sociality 51 (1986): 1069-1074.

Sullivan, Harry Stack. "The Interpersonal Theory of Psychiatry." in The Interpersonal Theory of Psychiatry. ed. Helen Perry and Mabel Gawel. New York: W. W. Norton & Company. (1953).

Unger, Donald and Abraham Wandersman. "The Importance of Neighbors: The Social, Cognitive, and Affective Components of Neighboring." American Journal of Community Psychology 13 (1985): 139-169.

Weiss, Robert. Loneliness: The Experience of Emotional and Social Isolation. Cambridge: MIT Press. 1973.

Wellman, Barry. "Structural Analysis: From Method and Metaphor to Theory and Substance." in Social Structures:A Network Approach, ed., Barry Wellman and S.D. Berkowitz. 19-61. Cambridge: Cambridge University Press, 1988.

_____. "Applying Network Analysis to the Study of Support." in Social Networks and Social Support, ed., Benjamin Gottleib. 171-200. Beverly Hills: Sage Publications, 1981.

_____, Carrington, Peter, and Alan Hall. "Networks as Personal Communities." in Social Structures: A Network Approach, ed., Barry Wellman and S. D. Berkowitz. 130-184. Cambridge: Cambridge University Press, 1988.

Williams, Janice and Cecilia Solano. "The Social Reality of Feeling Lonely: Friendship and Reciprocation." Personality and Social Psychology Bulletin 9 (1983): 237-242.

Woodward, Evelyn. Poets, Prophets, & Pragmatists: A Challenge to Religious Life. Notre Dame: Ave Maria Press. 1987.

GLOSSARY

Loneliness: While there are many definitions for loneliness, this study uses the definition given by Weiss coupled with the definition of Perlman and Peplau. "Loneliness is caused not by being alone but by being without some definite needed relationship or set of relationships . . ."[1] "that occurs when a person's network of social relations is deficient in some important way, either quantitatively or qualitatively."[2] Being without a needed relationship or set of relationships results in a great deal of anxiety and fear within the person. When the person's network is deficient, feelings of aimlessness,
marginality, and a sense that one does not belong occurs.[3]

Belonging: The individual feels a part of at least one significant group of others.

Spiritual well-being: Spiritual well-being is "the affirmation of life in relationship with God, self, community and environment that nurtures and celebrates wholeness."[4] This definition is broken into two parts, well-being in relationship to God (religious well-being), that is, one's sense of relatedness to God; and well-being in relationship to self and others (existential well-being), that is, a sense of life purpose and life satisfaction with no reference to anything specifically related to God. These definitions are used as a basis for the instrument that measures spiritual well-being.[5]

Spiritual loneliness: This term addresses a deficiency in a sense of spiritual well-being. "Cosmic/spiritual (sic) loneliness designates a sense of relatedness to God or a supreme being and a sense of relatedness to what the person believes to be his or her unique destiny in life".[6] It is a loneliness that results in an alienation from self, other, and God.

[1] Weiss, 17.
[2] Letitia Peplau and Dan Perlman, "Perspectives on Loneliness," in Loneliness: A Sourcebook of Current Theory, eds. Letitia Peplau and Dan Perlman (New York: John Wiley & Sons, 1982), p.4.
[3] Weiss.
[4] Paloutzian et al., 161.
[5] Ibid.
[6] Ami Rokach, "Theoretical Approaches to Loneliness: From a Univariate to a Multidimensional Experience," Review of Existential Psychology and Psychiatry 19 (1984-85): 236.

Social network: The operational definition used for this research is modeled on that of Hirsch:[7] a matrix formed by up to 15 significant others with whom they, the sample population, were likely to interact at least once during any two-week period.

Social support: Social/communal support (terms to be used interchangeably) is "an exchange of resources between at least two individuals perceived by the provider or the recipient to be intended to enhance the well-being of the recipient"[8] keeping in mind that there are negative and neutral relationships within a given network that influence our experience of support.[9]

Density: Density is the extent to which members of an individual's social network contact each other independently of the focal person.[10]

Size: The actual number of individuals with whom the focal person has direct contact.[11]

Reciprocity: The degree to which affective and instrumental aid; i.e., mutually confidential, is both given and received by the focal person.[12]

Religious Community: Community is a process of becoming united through a common experience of a core vision. The structure of the community is such that it serves to enable the members to carry out its vision and mission.[13]

---

[7] Barton Hirsch, "Psychological Dimensions of Social Networks: A Multimethod Analysis," American Journal of Community Psychology 7 (1979): 263-277.

[8] Sally Shumaker and Arlene Brownell, "Toward a Theory of Social Support: Closing Conceptual Gaps," Journal of Social Issues 40 (1984): 13.

[9] Marybeth Shinn et al., Social Interaction and Social Support, Journal of Social Issues 40 (1984): 55-76; Barry Wellman, "Applying Network Analysis to the Study of Support," in Social Networks and Social Support, ed. Benjamin Gottleib (Beverly Hills: Sage Publications, 1981), 171-200.

[10] Hirsch.

[11] Ibid.

[12] Roger Mitchell and Edison Trickett, "Task Force Report: Social Networks as Mediators of Social Support: An Analysis of the Effects and Determinants of Social Networks," Community Mental Health Journal 16 (1980): 27-44.

[13] Evelyn Woodward, Poets, Prophets, & Pragmatists: A Challenge to Religious Life (Notre Dame: Ave Maria Press, 1987).

SUBJECT INDEX

AUTHORS INDEX

AAN - 8370